Reporting Child Abuse and Neglect in North Carolina

Third Edition   2013

Janet Mason

UNC
SCHOOL OF
GOVERNMENT

The School of Government at the University of North Carolina at Chapel Hill works to improve the lives of North Carolinians by engaging in practical scholarship that helps public officials and citizens understand and improve state and local government. Established in 1931 as the Institute of Government, the School provides educational, advisory, and research services for state and local governments. The School of Government is also home to a nationally ranked graduate program in public administration and specialized centers focused on information technology and environmental finance.

As the largest university-based local government training, advisory, and research organization in the United States, the School of Government offers up to 200 courses, webinars, and specialized conferences for more than 12,000 public officials each year. In addition, faculty members annually publish approximately 50 books, manuals, reports, articles, bulletins, and other print and online content related to state and local government. Each day that the General Assembly is in session, the School produces the *Daily Bulletin Online*, which reports on the day's activities for members of the legislature and others who need to follow the course of legislation.

The Master of Public Administration Program is offered in two formats. The full-time, two-year residential program serves up to 60 students annually. In 2013 the School launched MPA@UNC, an online format designed for working professionals and others seeking flexibility while advancing their careers in public service. The School's MPA program consistently ranks among the best public administration graduate programs in the country, particularly in city management. With courses ranging from public policy analysis to ethics and management, the program educates leaders for local, state, and federal governments and nonprofit organizations.

Operating support for the School of Government's programs and activities comes from many sources, including state appropriations, local government membership dues, private contributions, publication sales, course fees, and service contracts. Visit www.sog.unc.edu or call 919.966.5381 for more information on the School's courses, publications, programs, and services.

Michael R. Smith, DEAN
Thomas H. Thornburg, SENIOR ASSOCIATE DEAN
Frayda S. Bluestein, ASSOCIATE DEAN FOR FACULTY DEVELOPMENT
L. Ellen Bradley, ASSOCIATE DEAN FOR PROGRAMS AND MARKETING
Todd A. Nicolet, ASSOCIATE DEAN FOR OPERATIONS
Bradley G. Volk, ASSOCIATE DEAN FOR ADMINISTRATION

FACULTY

Whitney Afonso	Norma Houston	Kimberly L. Nelson
Trey Allen	Cheryl Daniels Howell	David W. Owens
Gregory S. Allison	Jeffrey A. Hughes	LaToya B. Powell
David N. Ammons	Willow S. Jacobson	William C. Rivenbark
Ann M. Anderson	Robert P. Joyce	Dale J. Roenigk
A. Fleming Bell, II	Kenneth L. Joyner	John Rubin
Maureen Berner	Diane M. Juffras	Jessica Smith
Mark F. Botts	Dona G. Lewandowski	Meredith Smith
Michael Crowell	Adam Lovelady	Carl W. Stenberg III
Leisha DeHart-Davis	James M. Markham	John B. Stephens
Shea Riggsbee Denning	Christopher B. McLaughlin	Charles Szypszak
Sara DePasquale	Kara A. Millonzi	Shannon H. Tufts
James C. Drennan	Jill D. Moore	Vaughn Mamlin Upshaw
Richard D. Ducker	Jonathan Q. Morgan	Aimee N. Wall
Joseph S. Ferrell	Ricardo S. Morse	Jeffrey B. Welty
Alyson A. Grine	C. Tyler Mulligan	Richard B. Whisnant

This publication was made possible by Grant Number G-1301NCCJA1 from the Children's Bureau, U.S. Department of Health and Human Services, to the N.C. Department of Public Safety/Governor's Crime Commission. Its contents are solely the responsibility of the author and do not necessarily represent the official views of the Administration for Children and Families, the Children's Bureau, or HHS.

Contents

Preface   ix

PART 1. INTRODUCTION

Chapter 1
Purposes of the Reporting Law   3
　　Notes   7

Chapter 2
History of the Reporting Law   9
　　Background   9
　　North Carolina Law   10
　　Current Law   12
　　Notes   12

PART 2. KEY DEFINITIONS

Chapter 3
Significance of the Definitions   17
   Notes   18

Chapter 4
The People Defined: Juvenile, Parent, Guardian, Custodian, and Caretaker   21
   Which Children Are Covered?   21
   Whose Conduct Is Covered?   22
   Notes   26

Chapter 5
The Conditions Defined: Neglect, Abuse, Dependency, and Maltreatment   29
   Neglect   31
      Lack of Proper Care and Supervision   31
      Inappropriate Discipline   32
      Abandonment   33
      Lack of Necessary Medical or Remedial Care   34
      Injurious Environment   36
      Illegal Placement   37
   Abuse   39
      Causing or Allowing Serious Injury   40
      Cruelty   40
      Sexual Abuse   41
      Emotional Abuse   43
      Contributing to Delinquency   44
   Dependency   44
   Maltreatment   45
   Difficulty in Applying the Definitions—An Example   46
   Notes   49

PART 3. RESPONSIBILITIES AND RIGHTS OF REPORTERS

Chapter 6
Who Must Report   57
  General Rule   57
  Confidential and Privileged Communications   58
    Attorneys   58
    Judges   59
    Religious Officials   61
    Researchers   62
  Summary   63
  Notes   64

Chapter 7
Deciding to Report   67
  Cause to Suspect   67
  Guidelines   69
  Notes   71

Chapter 8
How to Report   73
  What to Include   74
  Anonymous Reports   74
  Reports by Institutions   75
  Reports about a Child in Another State   75
  Reports about Missing Children   76
  Notes   77

Chapter 9
Legal Rights of the Reporter   79
  Confidentiality   79
  Immunity for Reporting, Cooperating, or Testifying   81
  Notification and Review   82
  Notes   84

Chapter 10

Consequences of Failing to Report   87

   Criminal Liability   87

   Civil Liability   88

   Other Consequences of Failing to Report   90

   Notes   91

PART 4. ASSESSMENT AND RESPONSE

Chapter 11

Social Services Procedures   97

   Screening   97

   Notification after a Report Is Made   99

      Notifying the Reporter   99

      Notifying Law Enforcement   100

      Notification When Report Involves Child Care   100

   Social Services Assessment   101

      Purpose of Assessment   101

      Starting the Assessment   101

      Steps in an Assessment   102

      Confidential Information   103

      Assessment Following a Child's Death   104

      Assessment in an Institutional Setting   104

   Law Enforcement's Role   105

   Social Services Action   105

      Immediate Removal of Child   105

      Protective Services   106

      Keeping the Family Together   106

   Notification Requirements at Conclusion of Assessment   108

      To the Reporter   108

      To the Parent, Guardian, Custodian, or Caretaker   109

      To the Central Registry   109

      To a Responsible Individual and the Responsible Individuals List   110

      To the State Department of Health and Human Services and the State Bureau of Investigation When a Child Care Facility Is Involved   111

   Confidentiality and Information Sharing   112

      Confidentiality Rule   112

      When Disclosure Is Allowed   112

   Notes   114

Chapter 12

Review Procedures 119
  Review of Decision to Screen Out a Report 119
  Informal Review of Department's Determination after an Assessment 120
  Formal Review of Case Decisions 120
    Requesting Formal Review 121
    Timing of Review 121
    Review Process and Conclusion 122
  Review of Agency Practices or Community Issues 122
    County Social Services Boards 122
    State Division of Social Services 123
    Community Child Protection Teams 123
  Notes 125

Chapter 13

Juvenile Court Procedures 127
  Abuse, Neglect, or Dependency Petition 127
  Prehearing Custody 128
  Court Representation 130
    Child's Guardian ad Litem 130
    Representation for Parents 131
  Stages in Juvenile Cases 131
    Adjudication 131
    Disposition 132
    Review Hearings 133
  Authority over Parents 133
  Notes 134

PART 5. ROLE OF OTHER AGENCIES

Chapter 14

Schools and School Personnel 139
  Reports to Social Services by School Personnel 139
  Cooperative Agreements 142
    Sample Provisions for Cooperative Agreements 143
  Reporting in Relation to License Suspension and Revocation 146
  Reporting Certain Criminal Acts 147
  Notes 148

Chapter 15

Health and Mental Health Professionals and Facilities   151

   Reporting   151

   Professional Ethics and Reporting Responsibilities   152

   "Baby Doe": Disabled Infants with Life-Threatening Conditions   155

   Substance-Exposed Infants   156

   Emergency Custody in Abuse Cases   158

     Procedures   158

     Time Limits and Juvenile Court Action   159

   Treating Child without Parent's Consent   160

   **Judicial Authority for Emergency Medical Treatment
     When Parent Objects**   161

   **Child Medical Evaluation Program/
     Child Family Evaluation Program**   163

   Notes   163

Conclusion   167

Appendix A. Articles 1 and 3 of the North Carolina Juvenile Code   169

Appendix B. Selected Internet Sites   189

   North Carolina—Governmental   189

   North Carolina—Non-Governmental   191

   Federal and National   191

Preface

The material in this book reflects legislative changes to the North Carolina Juvenile Code through the 2013 session of the North Carolina General Assembly. Since publication of the 2003 edition of this book, the reporting law itself has been amended twice. In 2005, the word "assessment" replaced the term "investigation" to describe actions taken by a county department of social services when it receives a report of suspected abuse, neglect, dependency, or death by maltreatment. In 2013, the legislature for the first time provided criminal penalties for knowingly or wantonly failing to make a report, or preventing someone else from making a report, when the statute requires one. Changes in related laws and some court decisions also contribute to the need for this new edition.

This book should be a useful reference for teachers, counselors, principals, and other school personnel; mental health professionals; nurses, doctors, and other medical personnel; law enforcement officials; child care providers; and social workers. But the information in this book is important for everyone in North Carolina, regardless of profession, because the reporting law it discusses applies to everyone. The book may be useful as a training aid. It focuses on the law, however, and does not attempt to address such topics as medical and psychological indicators of abuse and neglect. Those subjects also should be considered critical components of training in this area.

The purposes of the book are

- to help readers understand when they are required to make reports;
- to explain how to make a report—both when the law requires that a report be made and when, even though a report is not required legally, a person feels that one should be made;
- to describe what happens after someone makes a report;
- to answer some of the questions people ask frequently about the reporting law; and
- to provide broader access to the exact wording of the reporting law and related statutes.

Readers should recognize that while the laws relating to child abuse and neglect are important, these are not primarily legal problems. Neither are they problems that can be addressed solely through county social services departments and the juvenile courts. This book is written with the hope that those who read it will be better informed about the reporting law and more aware that the responsibility for protecting children belongs to whole communities.

A grant from the Governor's Crime Commission of the North Carolina Department of Public Safety provided financial support for the production and distribution of this book. The School of Government greatly appreciates the commission's contribution to making this information widely available in the state. Many School of Government staff members contributed to the production of this book. If I tried to name them all I surely would omit someone whose contributions have been critical. All of them have my deep appreciation.

Janet Mason
Adjunct Professor
School of Government
The University of North Carolina at Chapel Hill
November 2013

Part 1. Introduction

"Any person or institution who has cause to suspect that any juvenile is abused, neglected, or dependent . . . or has died as the result of maltreatment, shall report the case of that juvenile to the director of the department of social services in the county where the juvenile resides or is found." [G.S. 7B-301]

Chapter 1

Purposes of the Reporting Law

A seventh-grade student comes to school with a badly swollen black eye. The teacher talks privately with the student, who says: "My dad hit me 'cause I broke his radio."

A teenager tells her best friend that her mother's live-in boyfriend has been coming into her room at night and touching her. She's afraid of him and afraid to tell her mother. The friend tells her own mother about the conversation.

A police officer picks up a four-year-old child he sees walking alone on the side of the road at night.

Parents tell a doctor that their son's injuries occurred when he tripped on a toy and fell down some stairs. The doctor thinks that explanation is inconsistent with the nature of the child's injuries.

In each of these examples, someone—a teacher, a parent, a law enforcement officer, a doctor—has a legal duty to make a report about a child's situation or condition. Most likely, even without a legal obligation to report, each of these people would do something to bring appropriate attention to the child's need for protection.

Historically, our system of justice has distinguished between moral obligations and legal duties. In the absence of a statute or a special relationship, private citizens are not obligated legally to involve themselves in other people's problems. North Carolina law includes neither a general mandate to report crimes nor a general mandate to report crimes involving child victims.[1] (Obviously, despite the absence of a legal duty to do so, many people do report these and other crimes to law enforcement officials when they know about them.) The legislature, however, has created reporting requirements directed to specific professions or groups of people, and some of these create a duty to report certain crimes.[2]

The reporting law discussed in this book is not a crime-reporting statute, and it applies to everyone, not just people in specific professions or relationships. By enacting this law, the North Carolina General Assembly has expressed a strong public policy of intervention on behalf of children whose parents or other care providers neglect them, inflict harm on them, place them at substantial risk of harm, or lack the ability to provide proper care for them. (For definitions of key terms specifying the kinds of harm or risk that must be reported, see Chapter 5.)

Although the circumstances that trigger a duty to report under this law often involve criminal offenses, the subject of the required report is not the criminal conduct or the person who commits it. It is the child who has been harmed or placed at risk of being harmed by that conduct. The reporting statute is part of the state's child protective services system, designed to respond to children's needs for protection or assistance in specified circumstances.[3] Because reporting is required in order to ensure that children receive the services and protection they need, the law requires reports to county departments of social services, not to law enforcement agencies. Sometimes the nature of a report that a social services department receives or the evidence that it finds in responding to a report generates a duty on the part of the department to make a report to law enforcement.[4] But the public's legal duty is to report to the department of social services.

The child protective services system is based on a body of law and procedures that are carried out primarily by county departments of social services and the juvenile (district) courts. These laws are in the North Carolina Juvenile Code (the Code), which establishes civil (as opposed to criminal) procedures for responding to children who are abused, neglected, or dependent.[5] The Code requires county social services departments to conduct assessments of reported cases of suspected child abuse, neglect, dependency, and death due to maltreatment and to offer services to children and families when those conditions are found to exist. It authorizes social services departments to take steps to protect children in emergencies and to begin juvenile court proceedings when necessary. The Code also defines the court's authority to adjudicate (make a legal determination) that a child is abused, neglected, or dependent and to order appropriate responses to meet the child's needs.

The United States Supreme Court has characterized parents' rights to care for and make decisions about their children as "fundamental" and has stated that these rights require heightened protection against government interference.[6] Parents are presumed to act in their children's best interest, and ordinarily there is no reason for the government to intervene in the private realm of a family.[7] The Supreme Court has said, for example, that "the Due Process Clause does not permit a State to infringe on the fundamental right of parents to make child rearing decisions simply because a state judge believes a 'better' decision could be made."[8]

When a child is harmed or placed at risk of harm by a stranger or by someone else who does not have caretaking responsibility for the child, we assume that the parent or other person responsible for the child's care will respond appropriately to meet the child's needs and keep the child safe. We rely on law enforcement, the criminal justice system, the juvenile justice system, employers, and others to respond appropriately to the conduct of the person who harmed the child or created the risk. Separate from the criminal justice system, the Juvenile Code provides for governmental intervention into the lives of the child and the child's family only when the parents, or people whose roles resemble those of parents,

- cause harm or risk of harm to the child,
- allow others to harm the child or put the child at risk,
- respond inappropriately when the child is harmed or placed at risk, or
- are unable or unwilling to prevent harm or risk of harm to the child or to care properly for the child.

The Juvenile Code balances opposing interests, defining the parameters of permissible state intervention into the lives of families and children for the purpose of protecting children. The Code identifies situations in which the state's interest in protecting children outweighs parents' rights to privacy and to freedom from governmental interference in the care of their children. Because the state's deference to these familial rights has constitutional dimensions, the threshold for state intervention must be carefully drawn.[9]

Sometimes social services departments are portrayed as doing too much in the name of protective services and intruding on families' rights without sufficient cause.[10] When a child is harmed or dies as a result of abuse or neglect, however, questions often arise as to why the protective services system failed to protect the child.[11] The children in the examples at the beginning of this chapter may be harmed, or further harmed, if no one takes steps to examine their situations and provide the services and protection they need. North Carolina's mandatory reporting law attempts to ensure that notice will be taken and that the needs of children like these will not be overlooked. In these examples, though, it is possible that the seventh-grader received the black eye in a fight with another student before school, that the teenage girl lied to her friend about her mother's boyfriend, or that the doctor's impression is incorrect and the child really was injured when he tripped on a toy and fell down the stairs.

Reports are required based on cause to suspect that a child is abused, neglected, or dependent, and suspicions may turn out to be unfounded. In those instances, the resulting inconvenience, embarrassment, and other negative consequences for the parents of those children are inevitable costs of requiring steps to identify those children whose circumstances do require intervention. However, understanding the reporting law and appreciating its purposes can help minimize inappropriate reports that have similar negative consequences and divert limited resources away from children whose cases are properly reported.

Recent high-profile cases of alleged sexual abuse have heightened interest in child abuse reporting laws but also have revealed confusion about what those laws require.[12] Although every state has a child abuse reporting law, the laws vary greatly in terms of who must report, what must be reported, and to whom reports must be made. Unlike the North Carolina law, some states' laws require reporting crimes that involve child victims, and many require only specified professionals to make reports. Thus, conversations about the duty to report must occur in the contexts of specific state laws. In some states the heightened interest in child abuse reporting has resulted in questions about the sufficiency of the laws and proposals to change them.[13] Clarity about the purposes a state assigns to its reporting law is an essential element of assessing proposed changes to the law.

In North Carolina, the reporting law applies to everyone in the state. Everyone has a legal duty to intervene, to the limited extent of making a report to a county department of social services, on behalf of children who may be "abused," "neglected," or "dependent," as the General Assembly has defined those terms. It is unlawful to ignore this duty. Complying with the reporting law, however, requires close attention to the way those three conditions are defined.

Notes

1. See Ric Simmons, *Private Plea Bargains*, 89 N.C. L. Rev. 1125, 1152 (2011), noting that the Model Penal Code does not criminalize the nonreporting of crimes and that only two states—Ohio and South Dakota—do so. *See also* L. Poindexter Watts, "The Duty to Report a Crime," *School Law Bulletin* 17 (Summer 1986): 22–30.

2. *See, e.g.*, North Carolina General Statutes (hereinafter G.S.) § 115C-288(g) (school principal's duty to report certain acts to law enforcement and to t.   principal's superintendent); G.S. 90-21.20 (duty of physicians and hospitals to report to law enforcement certain wounds, injuries, and illnesses). The North Carolina General Statutes can be viewed online at www.ncga.state.nc.us/gascripts/Statutes/StatutesTOC.pl. *See also* Sandra Guerra Thompson, *The White-Collar Police Force: "Duty to Report" Statutes in Criminal Law Theory*, 11 Wm. & Mary Bill Rts. J. 3 (2002), http://scholarship.law.wm.edu/cgi/viewcontent.cgi?article=1313&context=wmborj (discussing a variety of state and federal reporting requirements applicable to specific groups of professionals).

3. The criminal justice system, on the other hand, focuses on apprehending, prosecuting, and punishing people who engage in criminal conduct. One incident may precipitate simultaneous criminal justice and protective services responses. Although the criminal justice system does not focus on the victim, criminal procedures may affect a child victim in several ways. A criminal investigation may involve multiple interviews of the child, the child may be required to testify in a criminal proceeding, the child may feel vindicated or fearful or confused about what happens in the criminal system, and the person who harmed the child may be removed from the home or otherwise isolated from the child as a result of the criminal proceeding.

4. *See* G.S. 7B-301 and -307.

5. The North Carolina Juvenile Code (the Code) is codified as Chapter 7B of the North Carolina General Statutes. The Code also establishes procedures for responding to children whose behavior is undisciplined or delinquent, for terminating parental rights, for the emancipation of minors, and for juvenile matters involving more than one state. The Code is available at www.ncga.state.nc.us/gascripts/Statutes/StatutesTOC.pl?Chapter=0007B.

6. *See, e.g.*, Troxel v. Granville, 530 U.S. 57 (2000); Moore v. City of E. Cleveland, 431 U.S. 494 (1977); Prince v. Massachusetts, 321 U.S. 158 (1944); Pierce v. Soc'y of Sisters, 268 U.S. 510 (1925); Meyer v. Nebraska, 262 U.S. 390 (1923).

7. *See, e.g.*, Parham v. J.R., 442 U.S. 584 (1979).

8. *Troxel*, 530 U.S. at 72–73.

9. *See, e.g., In re* Stumbo, 357 N.C. 279, 286, 582 S.E.2d 255, 260 (2003) (acknowledging both "the extraordinary importance of protecting children from abuse, neglect, or dependency" and "the limits within which governmental agencies may interfere with or intervene in the parent-child relationship").

10. *See, e.g.,* Greene v. Camreta, 588 F.3d 1011 (9th Cir. 2009) (holding (1) that a lengthy interview of a suspected child abuse victim at school by a social worker and law enforcement officer was a "seizure" that, without a warrant, court order, exigent circumstances, or parental consent, violated the Fourth Amendment and (2) that a social worker's exclusion of a mother from a medical examination of her child violated "clearly established familial rights" under the Fourteenth Amendment), *vacated, remanded on other grounds sub nom.* Camreta v. Greene, 131 S. Ct. 2020 (U.S. 2011); *Stumbo,* 357 N.C. 279, 582 S.E.2d 255 (involving parents' claim that a department of social services was not justified in conducting an investigation after receiving an anonymous report of suspected neglect).

11. See, for example, "N.C. Agencies Questioned about How the Zahra Baker Case was Handled," wbtv.com, Feb. 21, 2011, updated March 22, 2011, www.wbtv.com/global/story.asp?s=14070673. *See also* Hunter v. Transylvania Cnty. Dep't of Soc. Servs., 207 N.C. App. 735, 701 S.E.2d 344 (2010) (involving allegations, made in a wrongful death action filed after a child died as a result of shaken baby syndrome, that social services personnel were negligent in investigating and responding to reports that the child was being neglected), *review denied,* 365 N.C. 346, 717 S.E.2d 377 (2011).

12. Both the 2011 scandal involving child abuse allegations against a football coach at Penn State University and the earlier controversy about child abuse in the Catholic Church generated calls for expanding the population of people who are legally required to report child abuse. Since 1979, North Carolina law has defined that population as broadly as possible, requiring reports by any person or institution with cause to suspect that a child is abused, neglected, or dependent. However, North Carolina law would not require a report if abuse were caused by a coach or religious official in a nonresidential setting. That is not because of any limitation on who must report. It is because the definition of "abused juvenile," for purposes of the reporting law, does not include a child who is abused by someone other than a parent, guardian, custodian, or caretaker. (Definitions of these and other key terms are discussed in Chapters 3, 4, and 5.)

13. The National Conference of State Legislatures reported that by June 27, 2013, "[a]pproximately 119 bills in 37 states and the District of Columbia [had] been introduced in the 2013 legislative session on the reporting of suspected child abuse and neglect." National Conference of State Legislatures, "Mandatory Reporting of Child Abuse and Neglect: 2013 Introduced State Legislation," updated June 27, 2013, www.ncsl.org/issues-research/human-services/mandatory-rprtg-of-child-abuse-and-neglect-2013.aspx.

Chapter 2

History of the Reporting Law

Background

North Carolina first enacted a juvenile code and created a juvenile court system in 1919.[1] While much of this code established procedures for responding to delinquent conduct by young people, the law also gave the newly created juvenile court jurisdiction over any child who was neglected; who "engage[d] in any occupation, calling, or exhibition"; who was "in such condition or surroundings or . . . under such improper or insufficient guardianship or control as to endanger the morals, health or general welfare" of the child; or who was "dependent upon public support or . . . destitute, homeless or abandoned."[2] This wording is the precursor of the current law's definitions of *abused juvenile, neglected juvenile*, and *dependent juvenile*. The 1919 juvenile code did not include a reporting requirement relating to any category of children.

Enactment of a juvenile code and creation of the juvenile court system indicated a growing recognition of the need for governmental involvement on behalf of children whose basic needs were not being met adequately.[3] Not until the 1950s and 1960s, however, did child abuse and neglect begin to be recognized as a major medical and social phenomenon. In 1962, publicity about a new medical diagnosis—battered child syndrome—captured the attention of some professionals and, to a lesser extent, that of the general public.[4] Reports emerged about the frequent failure within the medical community to diagnose child abuse or to refer cases of abused children to appropriate authorities. This publicity captured lawmakers' attention as well, and state legislatures began to enact child abuse reporting statutes. By 1966, all states except one had enacted laws requiring physicians to report suspected child abuse or at least allowing them to do so without fear of liability.[5] Over time, those laws have been expanded both to require more people to make reports and to broaden the kinds of conditions or maltreatment that must be reported.[6]

Because reporting requirements are matters of state law, they differ from state to state. Since the enactment of the federal Child Abuse Prevention and Treatment Act (CAPTA) of 1974, states have been required, as a condition of receiving certain federal child welfare funds, both to have child abuse and neglect reporting laws and to include specified elements in their state law definitions of abuse and neglect.[7] As a result, states' reporting laws tend to have some elements in common, but they still vary widely with respect to what must be reported and who is required to report.[8]

North Carolina Law

In North Carolina, the law commonly called the child abuse reporting law is part of the Juvenile Code, which comprises Chapter 7B of the state's General Statutes (hereinafter G.S.). It provides that

[a]ny person or institution who has cause to suspect that any juvenile is abused, neglected, or dependent, as defined by G.S. 7B-101, or has died as the result of maltreatment, shall report the case of that juvenile to the director of the department of social services in the county where the juvenile resides or is found.[9]

This law has evolved from what began as an attempt to encourage people to report child abuse and neglect. North Carolina's first reporting law, enacted in 1965, did not mandate reporting.[10] Rather, it served the limited purposes of authorizing physicians, teachers, and certain other professionals to report when they had cause to believe that a juvenile was abused or neglected and guaranteeing these professionals immunity from civil or criminal liability if they made a report in good faith. Without this protection, doctors and some other professionals were constrained from reporting by legal and/or ethical confidentiality requirements. This reporting law required county departments of social services to investigate these voluntary reports. It also created an exception to the physician–patient privilege, which otherwise would have restricted or prohibited testimony by physicians in court proceedings involving abuse or neglect. The exception meant that when a report of abuse or neglect resulted in a legal proceeding, the privilege could no longer be used to exclude medical testimony or evidence of abuse or neglect. This first reporting law applied only when the abuse or neglect was of a child younger than sixteen.

In 1971, a new law replaced the 1965 statute. The 1971 law made some reporting mandatory and distinguished between the reporting duties of certain professionals and those of other citizens.[11] It required specified professionals to report if they had reasonable cause to suspect that a child was abused or neglected.[12] It required all other people to report, but only if they had actual knowledge that a child was abused. The legislature included in the 1971 law the following statement of its purpose in requiring people to report child abuse and neglect:

> The General Assembly recognizes the growing problem of child abuse and neglect and that children do not always receive appropriate care and protection from their parents or other caretakers acting in loco parentis. The primary purpose of requiring reports of child abuse and neglect as provided by this Article is to identify any children suspected to be neglected or abused and to assure that protective services will be made available to such children and their families as quickly as possible to the end that such children will be protected, that further abuse or neglect will be prevented, and to preserve the family life of the parties involved where possible by enhancing parental capacity for good child care.[13]

The 1971 law made the good-faith immunity provisions applicable to all reporters. It maintained the exception to the physician–patient privilege in child abuse and neglect cases and added a comparable exception to the husband–wife privilege.

The next version of North Carolina's reporting law came into effect as part of a new juvenile code that was enacted in 1979.[14] In this law the legislature did not distinguish between professionals and other persons. It required reporting by any person or institution that had cause to suspect that a child was abused or neglected. A 1993 amendment added a requirement that people and institutions make a report when they have cause to suspect that a child is dependent or that a child has died as the result of maltreatment.[15]

The amendment also added a requirement that the report include the names and ages of other children in the home if the person who made the report knew that information.[16]

Current Law

Since July 1, 1999, the effective date of the current Juvenile Code, the mandatory reporting law has been located in G.S. 7B-301.[17] The reporting requirement itself has not changed since 1993, although definitions of some of the key terms that determine when a duty to report exists have changed. (See Chapter 5 for legal definitions of "abused," "neglected," "dependent," and other key terms.)

In 2013, the General Assembly directed the state Division of Social Services in the Department of Health and Human Services to study the state's policies and procedures for reporting child abuse and to make recommendations for improving the process.[18] The results of this study or proposals from other sources can lead to further changes in the reporting law or related provisions of the Juvenile Code.

Now, the law requires every person or institution with cause to suspect that a child is abused, neglected, or dependent or that a child has died as a result of maltreatment to report that child's situation to the county department of social services in the county where the child resides or is found.

The reporting mandate sounds simple. However, it raises many issues of interpretation, even for those who know about the law and want to comply with it.

Notes

1. 1919 N.C. Pub. Laws ch. 97. This action was preceded by legislation aimed at removing juvenile offenders from adult correctional facilities. *See, e.g.,* 1907 Pub. Laws ch. 509 (establishing the Stonewall Jackson Manual Training and Industrial School, which opened in Cabarrus County in 1909) and 1917 N.C. Pub. Laws ch. 255 (establishing a similar facility for girls in Moore County).

2. 1919 N.C. Pub. Laws ch. 97, sec. 1.

3. For information about the national context in which child abuse and neglect reporting laws were enacted, see generally John E. B. Myers, *Child Protection in America: Past, Present and Future* (New York: Oxford University Press, 2006).

4. Battered child syndrome was described in C. Henry Kempe et al., "The Battered-Child Syndrome," *Journal of the American Medical Association* 181 (July 1962): 17.

5. Seth C. Kalichman, *Mandated Reporting of Suspected Child Abuse: Ethics, Law, & Policy*, 2nd ed. (Washington, D.C.: American Psychological Association, 1999), 15 (hereinafter *Mandated Reporting of Suspected Child Abuse*). Although Kalichman states that laws in all states except Hawaii required physicians to report, the law in effect in North Carolina at that time merely authorized physicians to report.

6. Kalichman, *Mandated Reporting of Suspected Child Abuse*, cited in full in note 5.

7. Enacted as Public Law Number 93-247, CAPTA has been rewritten and amended numerous times since 1974 and currently is codified at 42 U.S.C. §§ 5101 *et seq.*; 42 U.S.C. §§ 5116 *et seq.* Changes in CAPTA and its requirements are summarized in Senate Committee on Health, Education, Labor and Pensions, CAPTA Reauthorization Act of 2010 (report to accompany Senate Bill 3817), S. Rep. No. 111-378 (2010), www.gpo.gov/fdsys/pkg/CRPT-111srpt378/pdf/CRPT-111srpt378.pdf.

8. *See* U.S. Department of Health & Human Services, Administration for Children & Families, Child Welfare Information Gateway, "Mandatory Reporters of Child Abuse and Neglect," August 2012, www.childwelfare.gov/systemwide/laws_policies/statutes/manda.cfm.

9. North Carolina General Statutes (hereinafter G.S.) § 7B-301. The statute goes on to explain how reports may be made and to specify the information that must be included in a report. The North Carolina General Statutes can be viewed online at www.ncga.state.nc.us/gascripts/Statutes/StatutesTOC.pl.

10. 1965 N.C. Sess. Laws ch. 472.

11. 1971 N.C. Sess. Laws ch. 710.

12. *Id.* The specified professionals included "a physician, surgeon, dentist, osteopath, optometrist, chiropractor, podiatrist, physician-resident, intern, a registered or practical nurse, hospital administrator, Christian Science practitioner, medical examiner, coroner, social worker, law enforcement officer, or a school teacher, principal, school attendance counselor or other professional personnel in a public or private school."

13. 1971 N.C. Sess. Laws ch. 710, sec. 1.

14. 1979 N.C. Sess. Laws ch. 815, sec. 1.

15. 1993 N.C. Sess. Laws ch. 516, sec. 4.

16. *Id.*

17. S.L. 1998-202, sec. 6.

18. S.L. 2013-360, sec. 12C.7, available at www.ncleg.net/Sessions/2013/Bills/Senate/PDF/S402v7.pdf. Results of the study must be reported to the Joint Legislative Committee on Health and Human Services and the Fiscal Research Division by April 1, 2014.

Part 2. Key Definitions

Chapter 3

Significance of the Definitions

When a person has cause to suspect that a child is abused, neglected, or dependent or that a child has died as the result of maltreatment, that person must report the child's situation to the county department of social services in the county where the child resides or is found.

How do you know when a child is or may be an "abused juvenile," a "neglected juvenile," or a "dependent juvenile"? The Juvenile Code (the Code) defines these and other key terms.[1] The definitions are important because they determine

1. which children's situations must be reported to the county department of social services;
2. whether the county social services department has a duty, and the authority, to conduct an assessment of the child's situation when it receives a report; and
3. whether the district court has authority to intervene on the child's behalf.

A court also must apply these definitions when an action is filed to terminate a parent's rights on the basis that the parent has abused or neglected his or her child[2] or that the parent is, and is likely to remain, incapable of providing proper care and supervision for the child, such that the child is a dependent juvenile, and the parent does not have a suitable alternative child care arrangement.[3] In addition, the law making it a misdemeanor to contribute to a child's being abused or neglected uses the Juvenile Code's definitions of those terms.[4]

Policies issued by the Division of Social Services in the state Department of Health and Human Services provide some guidance for interpreting the definitions.[5] When juvenile court orders relating to abuse, neglect, or dependency are appealed, the North Carolina appellate courts may be called on to decide whether trial courts have interpreted and applied the definitions correctly in specific circumstances.[6] The appellate court decisions become precedent for interpreting the definitions prospectively.

The Juvenile Code defines abused, neglected, and dependent juveniles— children whose situations must be reported to social services—fairly broadly. At the same time, the definitions exclude some children whom almost everyone would consider to be abused or neglected. This is because the Code does not attempt to describe all situations in which children are harmed, in which families and children might benefit from services, or in which services should be offered to families. As discussed above, the reporting law is not designed to require reports of crimes against children. Instead, the Code establishes the scope of the government's authority to intervene in families (or family-like situations) for purposes of protecting children, regardless of whether the family wants services or assistance. The reporting law is tied directly to identifying for proper authorities the circumstances in which that kind of intervention may be needed and is justified. Criminal laws, not the Juvenile Code and its definitions, specify when conduct affecting a child should be treated as a crime.[7]

The definitions discussed here are also discussed in the publication *Abuse, Neglect, Dependency, and Termination of Parental Rights Proceedings in North Carolina.*[8]

Notes

1. The definitions appear in North Carolina General Statutes (hereinafter G.S.) § 7B-101 and are reproduced in full in Appendix A. The North Carolina General Statutes can be viewed online at www.ncga.state.nc.us/gascripts/Statutes/StatutesTOC.pl. The Juvenile Code does not define *maltreatment*, and no appellate court decisions have interpreted the part of the reporting law that requires a report when a child dies as the result of maltreatment.

2. G.S. 7B-1111(a)(1).

3. G.S. 7B-1111(a)(6).

4. G.S. 14-316.1.

5. *See* N.C. Department of Health & Human Services, Division of Social Services, "Maltreatment Screening Tools and Procedures," in Section 1407, Chapter VIII, of the Division of Social Services' online *Family Support and Child Welfare Manual*, http://info.dhhs.state.nc.us/olm/manuals/dss/csm-60/man/CS1407-05.htm#P581_66025. The entire manual and manuals for other social services programs can be accessed from http://info.dhhs.state.nc.us/olm/manuals/manuals.aspx?dc=dss.

6. The North Carolina Administrative Office of the Courts provides electronic access to opinions of the North Carolina Supreme Court and the North Carolina Court of Appeals from 1998 forward at http://appellate.nccourts.org/opinions/. Opinions are also available through the Findlaw service, which allows one to locate cases by using search terms. State supreme court opinions date from February 1997, http://caselaw.findlaw.com/court/nc-supreme-court/, and court of appeals opinions date from January 1997, http://caselaw.findlaw.com/court/nc-court-of-appeals/. Older opinions can be accessed through subscription online legal research tools such as Lexis and Westlaw. Traditional published volumes of cases are available at law school libraries and some county libraries, as well as at law firms and state agencies.

7. *See, e.g.*, Ostwalt v. Charlotte-Mecklenburg Bd. of Educ., 614 F. Supp. 2d 603, 608 (W.D.N.C. 2008) (citation omitted) (rejecting a claim that law enforcement officers were negligent for failing to report a teacher's abuse of a child to the department of social services, because "[a]buse by a person who is not a parent, guardian, caretaker, or custodian is outside DSS's jurisdiction and falls under North Carolina criminal law").

8. Kella W. Hatcher, Janet Mason, and John Rubin, *Abuse, Neglect, Dependency, and Termination of Parental Rights Proceedings in North Carolina* (Chapel Hill, N.C.: UNC School of Government, 2011), sec. 2.4. This book can be accessed in PDF form, free of charge, at http://shopping.netsuite.com/s.nl/c.433425/it.A/id.4228/.f.

Chapter 4

The People Defined: Juvenile, Parent, Guardian, Custodian, and Caretaker

Which Children Are Covered?

The reporting law applies to all juveniles. For purposes of the reporting law, a "juvenile" is a minor—anyone under the age of eighteen—who is not married, has not been emancipated, and is not in the armed forces.[1] (In this book, the term "child" is used interchangeably with "juvenile.") Legislatures in some states—but not in North Carolina—have explicitly made their child protection laws applicable to unborn children.[2] North Carolina's Juvenile Code (the Code) has not been interpreted as applying to children before birth.[3]

The only minors to whom the reporting law does not apply are those who are emancipated or in the armed services. An "emancipated minor" is someone under the age of eighteen who has been released legally from parental control and who has many of the same rights as an adult. In North Carolina a minor may become emancipated in only two ways. First, a minor is emancipated automatically if he or she marries. A minor may marry in this state, however, only if

- he or she is at least sixteen years old and has the written consent of (1) a parent who has full or joint legal custody of the minor or (2) a person, agency, or institution that has legal custody of the minor or is serving as the minor's guardian; or
- the minor is fourteen or fifteen years old, the minor and the person he or she plans to marry are the parents of a child (whether born or

unborn), and the minor has filed a civil court action and obtained a court order authorizing the marriage.[4]

If a minor were to marry in another state, the validity of the marriage would depend primarily on whether the marriage conformed with the law of the other state.[5] For purposes of emancipation, it does not matter where the marriage occurred, if it is a valid marriage.

The second way a minor may become emancipated in North Carolina is by bringing an action in juvenile (district) court for a decree of emancipation.[6] Only sixteen- and seventeen-year-olds may seek court-ordered emancipation. A judge may grant an emancipation petition only after (1) the minor's parents are given notice, (2) a court hearing is held at which the judge makes extensive inquiries about the minor's circumstances, and (3) the judge concludes that emancipation is in the minor's best interest. This procedure and marriage are the exclusive means of emancipation in North Carolina.

The reporting law, therefore, covers all unmarried children under the age of eighteen except those in the armed services or with a legal court decree of emancipation. Minors may be abused, neglected, or dependent, and the subjects of mandatory reports, even if they

- have given birth or fathered children,
- live independently away from home,
- are treated by their parents as if they were emancipated, or
- declare themselves emancipated and are self-supporting.

Whose Conduct Is Covered?

The Juvenile Code defines "abused," "neglected," and "dependent juveniles" in terms of the effect or potential effect on children of the conduct or care-taking abilities of parents, guardians, custodians, or caretakers. A child who suffers an injury as a result of inappropriate discipline by a parent, guardian, custodian, or caretaker is an abused or neglected juvenile. A child who suffers an identical injury as a result of identical conduct by a schoolteacher, an older child, or a stranger is not an abused or neglected juvenile for purposes of the Juvenile Code and the reporting law.

A *parent*, although the Code does not define the term, may be a child's biological or adoptive parent, a person who is legally presumed to be a child's parent, or a person who has been determined by a court to be a child's parent.

A child's parent is considered the child's "natural guardian."[7] Otherwise, a guardian is someone appointed by a court to have the care, custody, and control of a child or to arrange an appropriate placement for the child.[8] A guardian also has the authority to consent on the child's behalf to medical care and other matters for which a parent's consent ordinarily would be required. The precise scope of a guardian's authority is determined by the statute under which the guardian is appointed and specific provisions in the court order appointing the guardian.[9] In North Carolina a guardian for a minor can be appointed in two ways:

1. The clerk of superior court, in a special proceeding, may appoint a "guardian of the person" or "general guardian" for a child, but only if the child either (1) has no natural guardian, that is, no parent; or (2) is adjudicated incompetent within the six months before the juvenile's eighteenth birthday.[10] Children ordinarily cannot be adjudicated incompetent. However, when it is clear that a minor will need a guardian when he or she becomes an adult, an adjudication is permitted during this six-month period so that a guardian will be in place when the minor reaches age eighteen.

2. In a juvenile court proceeding in which a juvenile is alleged or has been found to be abused, neglected, dependent, undisciplined, or delinquent, the district court may appoint a guardian of the person for the juvenile if (1) no parent appears at the hearing with the juvenile, or (2) the court finds the appointment would be in the juvenile's best interest.[11]

A "custodian" is a person or agency that has legal custody of a child—that is, custody pursuant to a court order.[12] Before October 1, 2013, a custodian also could be a person who has assumed the status and obligations of a parent but has not been awarded legal custody by a court.[13] A person in that role sometimes is called a *person in loco parentis*, a term the Juvenile Code does not use although it is still used in many other contexts to refer to someone who has assumed the role of a parent.[14] For purposes of the Juvenile Code, a person who assumes the role of a parent but does not have legal custody is a "caretaker," as discussed below.

A "caretaker" is someone (other than a parent, guardian, or custodian) who is responsible for a child's health and welfare in a residential setting.[15] A caretaker might be a stepparent, a foster parent, an adult member of the child's household, or an adult relative who has been entrusted with or voluntarily assumed responsibility for the child's care. People such as house parents or cottage parents who supervise children in residential child care facilities and residential schools also are caretakers. The Juvenile Code's definition of the term specifically includes any employee or volunteer of a division, institution, or school operated by the state Department of Health and Human Services.[16]

Because the definition of caretaker refers to someone responsible for a child's care "in a residential setting," the term does not encompass schoolteachers, coaches, club leaders, and others with similar temporary responsibility for children. (An exception relating to care providers in child care facilities is described below.) A babysitter or a girlfriend or boyfriend who does not live in the child's home generally would not be considered a caretaker.[17] If someone suspects that one of these non-caretakers has harmed or neglected a child or placed a child at risk, the law does not require that person to make a report to the department of social services. Still, most people who are aware of such an instance would take steps to ensure that the child receives proper attention and that the individual does not pose a threat to other children.[18] Appropriate responses might include one or more of the following:

- notifying the child's parents, guardian, or custodian, who presumably would respond to the child's medical needs and need for future care and protection;
- contacting law enforcement authorities;
- informing the individual's employer or supervisor or, if in a position to do so, taking appropriate personnel action.

Organizations and institutions that involve non-caretakers in regular contact with children often have their own internal policies or administrative requirements for reporting any individual who harms a child, places a child at risk, or acts inappropriately in relation to a child. Generally these reports would be made within the organization or to law enforcement or both.

If a person does make a report to a county department of social services about a non-caretaker, the department is not authorized to conduct an assessment, and it will not do so. However, if the report describes criminal conduct that results in physical harm to a child, the law requires the social services department to relay the information to the district attorney's office and to law enforcement officials.[19]

In an exception to the general requirement that a caretaker must be someone responsible for a child's care in a residential setting, the legislature has included within the meaning of caretaker people who are responsible for a child's care in a child care facility.[20] Except for child care arrangements that are specifically excluded by statute, "child care facility" is a child care center or home "where three or more children less than 13 years old, who do not reside where the care is provided, receive care on a regular basis of at least once per week for more than four hours but less than 24 hours per day from persons other than their guardians or full-time custodians, or from persons not related to them by birth, marriage, or adoption."[21]

The legal definition of "child care" exists primarily for licensing and regulatory purposes.[22] Someone caring for a child in a child care center or home ordinarily will be considered a caretaker. People who provide care for children but are not caretakers for purposes of the reporting law, because the places in which they care for children are excluded from the definition of child care, include those in

- public schools;
- recreation programs that operate for fewer than four consecutive months;
- organized clubs such as Boy Scouts, Girl Scouts, 4-H groups, and Boys and Girls Clubs; and
- drop-in or short-term care provided in health spas, resort hotels, bowling alleys, shopping malls, or churches.[23]

Someone who has primary responsibility for a child's care in a child care facility is a caretaker, and so is anyone who has that person's approval to assume responsibility for children who are in the primary provider's care. This might be an employee or a relative the provider asks to supervise or otherwise provide care for the children.

Observing or suspecting that a child has been injured or mistreated does not necessarily trigger a duty to make a report to the county department of social services. In order for a report to be required, and in order for the social services department to have the authority and responsibility to conduct an assessment, there must be cause to suspect that the child's condition can be attributed to the child's parent, guardian, custodian, or caretaker. If abuse or neglect occurs when a child is in the care of more than one parent, guardian, custodian, or caretaker, it is not necessary to know, or even to have cause to suspect, which of those persons is responsible for the child's abuse or neglect before making a report.

A child who is assaulted by an older juvenile, sexually molested by a stranger, or disciplined in a cruel manner by a schoolteacher would not come within the reporting requirement—unless, of course, there was also some indication that the child's parent (or guardian, custodian, or caretaker) allowed, contributed to, or responded inappropriately to the injury, harm, or risk to the child.

This is not to say that a concerned person has no recourse in these situations. Cases involving people who are not parents, guardians, custodians, or caretakers may be the subject of criminal investigations and prosecutions. They should be reported to law enforcement officials or to other appropriate authorities. These cases, however, do not come within the Juvenile Code provisions aimed at protecting children in family, family-like, and child care settings.

Notes

1. North Carolina General Statutes (hereinafter G.S.) § 7B-101(14). The North Carolina General Statutes can be viewed online at www.ncga.state.nc.us/gascripts/Statutes/StatutesTOC.pl.

2. *See, e.g.,* WIS. STAT. §§ 48.02(1)(am) (defining "abuse" to include, when "referring to an unborn child, serious physical harm inflicted on the unborn child, and the risk of serious physical harm to the child when born, caused by the habitual lack of self-control of the expectant mother of the unborn child in the use of alcohol beverages, controlled substances or controlled substance analogs, exhibited to a severe degree") and 48.133 (giving the court jurisdiction over certain unborn children and their expectant mothers). *See also* U.S. Department of Health & Human Services, Administration for Children & Families, Child Welfare Information Gateway, "Parental Drug Use as Child Abuse: Summary of State Laws," July 2012, www.childwelfare.gov/systemwide/laws_policies/statutes/drugexposed.pdf.

3. *See* N.C. Department of Health & Human Services, Division of Social Services, "The Impact of Drug and Alcohol Abuse," *in* Section 1440.XI, Chapter VIII, of the Division of Social Services' online *Family Support and Child Welfare Manual* (hereinafter *State Manual*), http://info.dhhs.state.nc.us/olm/manuals/dss/csm-60/man/CS1440-10.htm#P213_31521 (stating that North Carolina child protective services laws do not address abuse or neglect of the unborn child).

Some North Carolina appellate court decisions refer to findings of fact by the trial court about a mother's drug use during pregnancy, but these findings have not been the subject of appellate court decisions. Typically these findings relate to the issue of whether there is a likelihood of future abuse or neglect. *See, e.g., In re* K.P.M., ___ N.C. App. ___, 680 S.E.2d 901 (2009) (unpublished) (holding that the trial court's finding of a high likelihood that neglect would be repeated if the children were returned to the mother was supported by evidence showing, among other things, that the mother had used cocaine while pregnant with one child, after two other children had been removed from the home because of her substance abuse, and that all three children had tested positive for cocaine).

4. G.S. 51-2(a1) and -2.1(a). *See* G.S. 7B-3509 (stating that marriage for a minor translates into emancipation). North Carolina's marriage laws are available for viewing at www.ncga.state.nc.us/gascripts/Statutes/StatutesTOC.pl?Chapter=0051. *See also* Janet Mason, "Marriage in North Carolina," *Popular Government* 71 (Winter 2006): 26–36, www.sogpubs.unc.edu/electronicversions/pg/pgwin06/article3.pdf.

5. *See* 1 SUZANNE REYNOLDS, LEE'S NORTH CAROLINA FAMILY LAW § 2.14 (5th ed. 1993 & Supp. 2010).

6. *See* Article 35 of G.S. Chapter 7B (G.S. 7B-3500 through -3509).

7. *See* G.S. 35A-1201(a)(6).

8. A court appoints a "guardian ad litem," on the other hand, only to represent a child's interest in a particular civil court action. *See, e.g.,* G.S. 7B-601 and 1A-1, Rule 17. "Guardian," except when referring to a parent's natural status, denotes a status created by and subject to change by a court order. In one context, however, a court held that a relative was a guardian even though no court action had occurred. *See* State v. Jones, 147 N.C. App. 527, 556 S.E.2d 644 (2001) (holding that the custodial interrogation of a juvenile did not violate the juvenile's *Miranda* rights because the juvenile's aunt was present and was the juvenile's guardian within the meaning and spirit of the juvenile interrogation statute, even though she had not been appointed by a court as the juvenile's guardian), *review denied*, 355 N.C. 351, 562 S.E.2d 427 (2002).

9. *See* G.S. 7B-600 and -2001 and G.S. 35A-1240 to -1245.

10. G.S. 35A-1203(a), -1105. The clerk may appoint a "guardian of the estate" for any minor who has assets or property. G.S. 35A-1203(a). A general guardian is one who serves as both guardian of the person and guardian of the estate.

11. G.S. 7B-600, -2001. Despite the breadth of the statute's wording, appointment of a guardian based solely on a "best interest" determination is unlikely. Parents have a constitutionally protected interest in the care and custody of their children, and before awarding custody to someone other than a parent or appointing a guardian of the person for a minor, a court must find that the parent is unfit, has neglected the child's welfare, or has acted inconsistently with the parent's constitutionally protected parental status. *See, e.g., In re* B.G., 197 N.C. App. 570, 574, 677 S.E.2d 549, 552 (2009) (citations omitted) (stating that "to apply the best interest of the child test in a custody dispute between a parent and a nonparent, a trial court must find that the natural parent is unfit or that his or her conduct is inconsistent with a parent's constitutionally protected status").

12. G.S. 7B-101(8).

13. The definition of "custodian" in G.S. 7B-101(8) was rewritten by S.L. 2013-129, sec. 1, to delete this category of custodian effective October 1, 2013.

14. *See, e.g.,* G.S. 50-13.4(b) (specifying secondary liability for child support); G.S. 50B-2(c) (providing for ex parte orders in domestic violence actions); G.S. 115C-369(b) (addressing applications for school reassignment); and G.S. 122C-3(20) (defining "legally responsible person" for purposes of mental health, developmental disabilities, and substance abuse services statutes).

15. G.S. 7B-101(3).

16. *Id.*

17. "Structured Intake," in Section 1407, Chapter VIII, *State Manual,* cited in full in note 3, 4–5, http://info.dhhs.state.nc.us/olm/manuals/dss/csm-60/man/CS1407.pdf.

18. Some professionals may be constrained by confidentiality requirements from reporting these cases if the law does not require them to make a report.

19. G.S. 7B-307(a). The social services director must make immediate oral reports and subsequent written reports to both the district attorney and the appropriate local law enforcement agency.

20. G.S. 7B-101(3).

21. G.S. 110-86(2) and (3).

22. G.S. 110-86(2).

23. *Id.*

Chapter 5

The Conditions Defined: Neglect, Abuse, Dependency, and Maltreatment

This chapter may leave readers frustrated, because it will not answer some of the questions they want answered. When someone describes a child's situation and asks whether the child is an abused, neglected, or dependent juvenile and whether a report must be made, a quick yes or no answer often is not possible. The answer may be, "It depends," or simply, "It isn't clear." People trying to decide whether to make reports should not assume that they are alone in being uncertain about the applicability of particular terms.

The question of whether a given set of facts constitutes "abuse," "neglect," or "dependency" may be asked at several stages in a child protective services case, and it is not unusual for the question to be answered differently at different stages. To some extent that is because the degree of certainty required is not the same at every stage. For example, a person who has only "cause to suspect" that a child is abused, neglected, or dependent must make a report;[1] however, in order for a court to conclude that a child is abused, neglected, or dependent, the court must make findings based on "clear and convincing evidence."[2] In addition, at each stage a different person or entity is called on to interpret and apply the key definitions, and additional information usually becomes available as the case proceeds. Still, people with the same information at the same time may reach different conclusions, because the definitions are not very precise, and each person brings his or her own experiences, values, and perspectives to the question of whether abuse, neglect, or dependency exists.

Those who must interpret and apply the definitions, in addition to a person deciding whether to make a report, include the following:

1. county social services staff who screen a report by determining whether, if the information given in the report is true, the child is an abused, neglected, or dependent juvenile;
2. other social services staff who conduct an agency review if a report is screened out—that is, not accepted for purposes of conducting an assessment—and the person who made the report asks for a review of that decision;
3. a social worker who conducts an assessment and determines with others in the department how the findings should be characterized;
4. a prosecutor who is asked by the person who made a report to review a social services department's decision not to file a petition in juvenile court alleging that the child is an abused, neglected, or dependent juvenile;
5. a social services department's attorney advising the department about whether to file a petition or which condition(s) to allege in a petition;
6. a district court judge (or someone else to whom the chief district judge has delegated authority) deciding whether to grant a nonsecure custody order to remove a child from the home before a full hearing on a petition;
7. the guardian ad litem and attorney advocate appointed by the court to represent the child, and the parents and their attorneys, who must decide whether to contest a petition;
8. the district court judge who presides over the hearing on a petition alleging that a child is abused, neglected, or dependent;
9. a three-judge panel of the North Carolina Court of Appeals, when a district court judge's order in a juvenile case is appealed;
10. the North Carolina Supreme Court, when it reviews a decision of the court of appeals;
11. the parties and the court in a termination of parental rights proceeding, when the petition includes allegations that the parent has abused or neglected the child or that the child is dependent; and
12. a magistrate, a prosecutor, and others in a case involving the criminal offense of contributing to a child's being abused or neglected.

This chapter attempts to explain what is clear about the meaning of abuse, neglect, dependency, and maltreatment and to acknowledge some areas of uncertainty. The definitions of each of these conditions and their subparts are discussed below.

Neglect

The Juvenile Code (the Code) defines a "neglected juvenile" as a child who

- does not receive proper care, supervision, or discipline from the child's parent, guardian, custodian, or caretaker; or
- has been abandoned; or
- is not provided necessary medical care; or
- is not provided necessary remedial care; or
- lives in an environment that is injurious to the child's welfare; or
- has been placed for care or adoption in violation of law.[3]

The statutory definition also states that in determining whether a child is neglected, it is relevant whether the child lives in a home where another child has died as a result of suspected abuse or neglect or has been subjected to abuse or neglect by an adult who regularly lives in the home.

This definition has withstood judicial scrutiny when challenged on the ground that it was unconstitutionally vague.[4] In one case, the court found that the terms used in the definition are given "precise and understandable meaning by the normative standards imposed upon parents by our society."[5] The court said, in effect, that people can use common sense and generally accepted values to determine what is meant by "proper care," "necessary medical care," or "injurious environment."

Neglect may take a variety of forms, as described below.

Lack of Proper Care and Supervision

Neglect may consist of a parent's failure to provide for the child's basic needs.[6] It is not necessary, however, for a child to suffer physical harm or be threatened with physical harm in order to be neglected. For example, depriving a child of needed therapeutic day care has been found to be neglect.[7] Proper care and supervision include providing a child with a basic education, so a parent's willful failure to enroll a child in school can be neglect and require a report to social services.[8] When someone has concerns about a child's school attendance or about the quality or quantity of instruction a home-schooled child is receiving, contacting the appropriate school authority is an appropriate first step.[9] Anyone with cause to suspect that abuse or neglect is occurring in the home-school setting must make a report to the county department of social services.

Leaving a young child unsupervised may be neglect; however, the law does not specify any particular age below which a child is considered neglected if left at home alone. Rather, it assumes that parents and others will exercise appropriate discretion based not only on the child's age, but also on the child's maturity and all of the relevant circumstances.[10]

Whether a child is neglected based on a lack of proper care and supervision depends not only on the conduct of a parent, guardian, custodian, or caretaker, but also on the effect that conduct has or could have on the child. The child is neglected only if, as a result of that conduct, the child is harmed in some way or placed at substantial risk of harm.[11] The fact that a parent has serious mental health or substance abuse issues does not, by itself, mean that the parent's children are neglected. It is necessary to examine the parent's conduct in relation to the quality of the care and supervision the children receive and whether the children have been harmed or placed at substantial risk of harm by the parent's conduct.[12]

Inappropriate Discipline

Neglect may occur through a parent's failure to act or through a parent's actions. Inappropriate discipline that harms a child or creates a substantial risk of harm, if it is not severe enough to constitute abuse, is neglect. In the context of child protective services, excessive or inappropriate discipline constitutes abuse only if it causes (or creates a substantial risk of) serious physical injury or involves the use of cruel or grossly inappropriate procedures or devices.[13]

The North Carolina Court of Appeals held that a five-year-old child was neglected on the basis that her mother had hit her in the face with a belt, causing bruises, and had scrubbed her so hard during bathing (as discipline for the child's sexual curiosity) that the child bled.[14] In another case, the court upheld a neglect adjudication where evidence showed, among other things, that the mother struck her one-year-old child with a belt, "raising the distinct potential of physical, mental, or emotional harm."[15] Other examples of neglect in the form of inappropriate discipline have included hitting a young child with a paddle on the soles of the child's feet,[16] forcing a child to stay in an uncomfortable position for an extended period of time, inflicting numerous whippings with switches or boards, and forcing a child to spend weekends in bed and to get out of bed only to go to the bathroom or eat.[17]

Where a parent's actions clearly constitute inappropriate discipline that is harmful or potentially harmful to the child, it is not important for the person making a report to be certain whether the child's condition is one of abuse or of neglect. The duty to report is the same.

Almost any method of disciplining a child—time out, taking away privileges, spanking—can be inappropriate and harmful if taken too far. But how far is too far? The court of appeals has stated the following rule of thumb: "In general, treatment of a child which falls below the normative standards imposed upon parents by our society is considered neglectful."[18] That rule can be difficult to apply. Strongly held beliefs about what constitutes proper discipline can vary greatly among parents, communities, religious groups, and cultures.[19]

Abandonment

The courts have described *abandonment* as a parent's willful refusal to perform a parent's natural and legal obligations to care for and support a child, and also as a parent's willful conduct that shows an intent to forego all of the parent's duties and rights in relation to the child.[20] The fact that one parent abandons a child does not necessarily mean that the child is a neglected juvenile. The parent's conduct must be connected to harm or a substantial risk of harm to the child, and often abandonment by one parent occurs when the child is receiving very adequate care from the other parent. Most appellate court decisions involving abandonment deal with proceedings to terminate a parent's rights, in which the issue is the *parent's conduct*, not the child's condition and need for intervention, protection, or services.[21]

The type of abandonment that must be reported occurs, for example, when a newborn is left in a basket on the steps of a church, when a mother leaves the hospital after giving birth and cannot be found, or when a parent leaves a child with a temporary caregiver and does not return. The Juvenile Code contemplates this kind of abandonment when it requires a county department of social services to act immediately when it receives a report that a child has been abandoned.[22] The department is required to begin an assessment, assume custody of the child, file a petition, and seek a court order allowing the department to retain custody pending a hearing. The department also must ask law enforcement to investigate through state and national resources to determine whether the abandoned child has been reported missing.[23]

Publicity about cases in which a parent killed a newborn infant or abandoned the newborn in an unsafe place, often after the mother had hidden her pregnancy from family and friends, has led a number of states to enact legislation aimed at deterring such acts. In 2001, the North Carolina General Assembly enacted legislation to shield from criminal prosecution a parent who, within the first seven days of a child's life, voluntarily leaves the child with another person and does not express an intent to return for the child.[24] The law requires certain professionals, and allows any other person, to accept physical custody of the infant in that situation. It requires the person receiving the child to take certain actions, including contacting the county department of social services or law enforcement authorities immediately.[25] A social services department receiving a report of a parent's abandonment of a child in this way must begin an assessment immediately and proceed as in any other case of reported neglect.

Lack of Necessary Medical or Remedial Care

Necessary medical care and *necessary remedial care* have not been defined precisely. A court had no trouble concluding that a child was neglected when the child's father had both failed to seek treatment for the child's serious burns and refused to allow a social worker to do so.[26] Where parents failed to obtain medical care for their four-month-old child until at least three weeks after he suffered four broken ribs, the child was found to be both abused and neglected.[27]

Other deprivations of medical or remedial care may be less obvious, but this form of neglect clearly extends beyond physical harm. The court of appeals affirmed a finding of neglect based on a mother's refusal to allow treatment for her child's severe hearing and speech defects.[28] In that case, the court of appeals said, "To deprive a child of the opportunity for normal growth and development is perhaps the greatest neglect a parent can impose upon a child."[29]

North Carolina is among a minority of states with reporting laws that do not address parents' religious beliefs as the asserted reason for not seeking or consenting to medical care or treatment for a child. The definitions of child abuse and neglect in thirty-one states include explicit exceptions for circumstances in which parents do not seek medical care for their children because of their religious beliefs, but many of those states also have laws that authorize the court to order medical treatment for a child over the parents' objections.[30]

In North Carolina, courts consider these issues as they are raised in individual cases, but no reported appellate court decisions involve allegations of medical neglect based on a parent's religious objections to obtaining treatment for a child. Courts generally would defer greatly, but not completely, to parents' wishes regarding the medical care their children receive. In one case, after children were adjudicated neglected for reasons unrelated to medical care and placed in the custody of social services, the trial court ordered that the children be immunized despite the parents' religious objections. The North Carolina Court of Appeals upheld the order, saying, "Our courts do not have a history of routinely ordering the performance of medical procedures on children without parental consent. However, when parents refuse to provide necessary medical care, their inaction can extinguish custody and support a finding of neglect."[31]

In another case, the court of appeals rejected a father's claim that his refusal to permit a mental health evaluation of his children during an abuse investigation was lawful because he objected to the evaluation on religious grounds. The court said the following:

> One may not be compelled by governmental action to do that which is contrary to his religious belief in the absence of a 'compelling state interest in the regulation of a subject within the State's Constitutional power to regulate'. . . . The intent of the statutes requiring the Department of Social Services to screen and investigate complaints of child abuse is the protection of neglected and abused children . . . which is undeniably a compelling state interest.[32]

A mother's strong, apparently non-religious, beliefs about medicine and diet led her to resist and interfere with her daughter's treatment for juvenile rheumatoid arthritis. The child became malnourished, lost a significant amount of weight, and suffered further damage to her joints, but she improved quickly when removed from her mother's custody. The appellate court, in an unpublished opinion, affirmed an adjudication that the twelve-year-old child was both abused and neglected.[33]

Medical neglect is not limited to the deprivation of medical or remedial treatment or care. Subjecting a child to inappropriate medical care also may be neglect, or abuse, or both. If inappropriate treatment causes or creates a substantial risk of serious physical injury to the child, it can be abuse. An adjudication of the abuse ground for terminating a parent's rights was affirmed when evidence showed that during a two-year period the mother regularly exaggerated the child's medical problems and "subjected the child to 25 different emergency room visits, 60 office visits to pediatricians, 143 prescriptions, and 8 admissions to the hospital."[34] A child was adjudicated to be both abused and neglected, and the court of appeals affirmed, when the child's symptoms appeared only when she was in her mother's exclusive care and repeated medical procedures showed no medical problem.[35]

A person deciding whether to make a report based on cause to suspect that a child is not receiving necessary medical care or is receiving inappropriate medical care or treatment need not be concerned about whether the child's condition is more appropriately characterized as neglect or as abuse. The duty to report is the same.

Injurious Environment

A child is neglected if the child lives in an environment that is injurious to the child's welfare. As with other forms of neglect, an injurious environment may be one that puts the child at substantial risk of harm as well as one in which the child actually has been harmed. An injurious environment might be one in which the child is at risk of physical harm due to faulty wiring, exposure to dangerous substances or objects, or an extreme lack of sanitation. The conduct of the adults in the home also can render an environment injurious. For example, the court of appeals affirmed a trial court's conclusion that a child whose older sister had been sexually abused in the home lived in an injurious environment.[36] A child who lives in an injurious environment ordinarily also is not receiving proper care or supervision from the child's parent, guardian, custodian, or caretaker, and the cases involving these two types of neglect often overlap.

The instability of a child's living situation can be a factor in a court's determination that the environment in which the child lives is injurious. A parent's inability to maintain secure living arrangements is relevant to a determination of whether a child is neglected.[37] In one case, the court held that frequent moves combined with the exposure of the child to drugs and violence constituted an injurious environment.[38]

Domestic violence in the home has been cited independently in support of a determination that an environment is injurious to a child.[39] Violence aimed at the child also may contribute to an environment's being injurious. In one case, the court held that a child's credible testimony that her father used forced sexual intercourse as discipline was sufficient to support a determination that she lived in an injurious environment and was neglected as well as abused.[40]

Substance abuse also is mentioned frequently, often in combination with other factors, in relation to injurious environments.[41] However, the presence or use of drugs or alcohol must be linked to harm or a risk of harm to the child in order for it to support or contribute to a determination that the child is neglected. In one case, the court found that a mother's severe problem with alcohol abuse created an injurious environment for her children.[42] The evidence and the court's findings addressed not only the severity of the mother's alcohol problem, but also the ways in which her conduct placed the children at risk and the fact that her drinking contributed to the older children's emotional problems.[43]

Illegal Placement

Placing a child illegally for care or adoption is a form of neglect, although one that is rarely the basis for court action. Several statutes govern the placement of children, however, and cause to suspect that a child's placement violates any of these statutes could form the basis of a duty to report. These include laws that specify licensing requirements for establishing, operating, or providing foster care for children and for receiving or placing children in residential care facilities, foster homes, or adoptive homes.[44] A child placed in a foster home by an agency that was not licensed as required by these laws, for example, might be neglected under this part of the definition.

A child also may be neglected if someone who is not legally authorized to place children for adoption places the child for that purpose. Under the state's adoption laws, a child may be placed for adoption in North Carolina only by

- a county department of social services;
- another legally authorized agency;

- the child's guardian (but not a guardian appointed in a juvenile proceeding or a guardian ad litem);
- both parents acting jointly; or
- one parent who has both legal and physical custody of the child (unless the parents are married and still living together).[45]

Another group of laws regulates bringing a child into North Carolina or sending a child from here to another state for placement in foster care or for adoption. Under the Interstate Compact on the Placement of Children,[46] it is unlawful to bring or send a child across state lines for this type of placement without providing the receiving state with certain information, receiving that state's determination that the proposed placement does not appear to be contrary to the child's interests, and complying with other requirements of the compact. These laws do not apply when a child's parent, guardian, or relative is placing the child with a parent, guardian, or specified relative in another state. A child's placement would violate the compact, though, if a parent, court, or agency in another state placed the child in an adoptive home in North Carolina without first obtaining a favorable home study from a North Carolina agency.

The adoption law makes it a misdemeanor to offer, pay, or accept money (or anything of value) either for the placement of a child for adoption or for a parent's consent to adoption, unless the payment is one specifically authorized by statute.[47] In addition, criminal statutes address human trafficking, which occurs when a person "knowingly recruits, entices, harbors, transports, provides, or obtains by any means another person with the intent that the other person be held in involuntary servitude or sexual servitude."[48] Until December 1, 2012, however, no North Carolina statute criminalized or specifically prohibited the selling of children, and it was not always clear which if any criminal offense occurred when someone did buy or sell a child.[49]

In 2012, the General Assembly created the offense of unlawful sale, surrender, or purchase of a child.[50] A person commits the offense if he or she, "acting with willful or reckless disregard for the life or safety of a child," participates in "the acceptance, solicitation, offer, payment, or transfer of any form of compensation in connection with the unlawful acquisition or transfer of physical custody of a child."[51] When the offense is committed or attempted by the child's parent, guardian, or custodian, the new statute provides explicitly that the child "is an abused juvenile for purposes of the Juvenile Code [G.S. 7B-101(1)] and [that] the court may place the child in the custody of a county department of social services or any person, as the court finds to be in the child's best interest."

Abuse

The Juvenile Code considers a child to be an "abused juvenile" when the child's parent, guardian, custodian, or caretaker acts in certain specified ways with respect to the child. Conduct covered by the definition falls into several main categories—physical abuse, emotional abuse, sexual abuse—and these may overlap in a given case.[52] Although abuse may take a variety of forms, the North Carolina Supreme Court has said that its fundamental nature, "based upon its statutory definition, is the existence or serious risk of some nonaccidental harm inflicted or allowed by one's caretaker."[53]

As defined in the Code, an abused juvenile is a child whose parent, guardian, custodian, or caretaker

- inflicts, or allows someone else to inflict, on the child a serious physical injury that is not accidental;
- creates, or allows someone else to create, a substantial risk that the child will suffer a serious physical injury that is not accidental;
- uses, or allows someone else to use, cruel or grossly inappropriate procedures or devices to modify the child's behavior;
- commits, or permits or encourages someone else to commit, any of a number of specified sexual offenses "by, with, or upon the juvenile";
- commits, permits, or encourages someone else to commit the offense of unlawfully selling, surrendering, or purchasing the child;
- creates, or allows someone else to create, serious emotional damage to the child;
- encourages, directs, or approves of delinquent acts involving moral turpitude committed by the child; or
- commits or allows someone else to commit an offense under G.S. 14-43.11 (human trafficking), G.S. 14-43.12 (involuntary servitude), or G.S. 14-43.13 (sexual servitude) against the child.[54]

Causing or Allowing Serious Injury

A child is abused, for purposes of the reporting law, if the child's parent, guardian, custodian, or caretaker inflicts—or allows someone else to inflict—on the child a serious, nonaccidental physical injury. A child also is abused if one of those persons creates—or allows to be created—a substantial risk of serious, nonaccidental physical injury to the child. The Juvenile Code does not define *serious physical injury*. However, the criminal statute that describes offenses constituting felony child abuse defines "serious physical injury" as a "[p]hysical injury that causes great pain and suffering" and specifies that it includes "serious mental injury."[55] The North Carolina Court of Appeals agreed with a trial court's determination that a three-year-old child had suffered a serious, nonaccidental physical injury and was an abused juvenile when a spanking resulted in a dark, six-inch bruise on the child's thigh, the child experienced discomfort for several days, and the bruise lasted for over a week.[56]

Serious physical injury does not have to be severe, but it must cause great pain and suffering or constitute a serious mental injury. Bruising alone will not always be sufficient to support a determination of abuse.[57] As explained above, however, a child who receives or is put at risk of a nonaccidental injury that is not serious enough to constitute abuse may be a neglected juvenile if the injury results from inappropriate care, supervision, or discipline.

Cruelty

A child is abused if the parent, guardian, custodian, or caretaker uses, or allows someone else to use, cruel or grossly inappropriate procedures or devices to modify the child's behavior. In an unpublished opinion, the court of appeals affirmed an adjudication that a child was abused based on the mother's "cruel or grossly inappropriate" disciplinary methods. The mother had forced the six-year-old child to stand holding his arms out by his side for up to five minutes at a time, or longer if his behavior did not improve; placed duct tape over the child's mouth; and struck the child with a belt, paddle, switch, or other object, causing injuries to his arms and legs.[58]

Trying to change a child's behavior by using electrical shocks, tying the child to a bedpost, depriving the child of food, or forcing the child to consume inordinate amounts of water are examples of the ways parents and others can abuse children in this manner. In appellate court decisions, instances of abuse in the form of cruelty show up in criminal appeals more often than in juvenile abuse or neglect cases.[59] If the person who harmed the child is out of the home and is charged with criminal child abuse, there may be no need for social services to initiate a juvenile court proceeding if the child is safe with the remaining parent, guardian, custodian, or caretaker.

Sexual Abuse

Sexual abuse, for purposes of the reporting law, occurs when a child's parent, guardian, custodian, or caretaker commits, permits, or encourages the commission by, with, or upon the juvenile of any of the criminal offenses listed below. When the child's age is relevant to whether the offense has occurred, that is indicated.

- First-degree rape (G.S. 14-27.2). Unless by force, the offense occurs only if the victim is younger than thirteen and the person committing the act is at least twelve and four years older than the victim.
- Second-degree rape (G.S. 14-27.3). Unless by force, the offense occurs only if the person committing the act knows or reasonably should know that the victim is mentally disabled, mentally incapacitated, or physically helpless.
- Rape of a child by an adult offender (G.S. 14-27.2A). The offense occurs if a person who is eighteen or older engages in sexual intercourse with a child younger than thirteen.
- First-degree sexual offense (G.S. 14-27.4). If not by force, the offense occurs only if the child is younger than thirteen and the person committing the act is at least twelve and at least four years older than the victim.
- Second-degree sexual offense (G.S. 14-27.5). If not by force, the offense occurs only if the person committing the act knows or reasonably should know that the victim is mentally disabled, mentally incapacitated, or physically helpless.
- Sexual offense with a child by an adult offender (G.S. 14-27.4A). The offense occurs if a person who is eighteen or older engages in a sexual act with a child younger than thirteen.
- Sexual act by a custodian or school personnel (G.S. 14-27.7).
    - Age is not a factor if the person committing the act has assumed the position of a parent in the child's home, has custody of the child, or is an agent or employee of a person or institution that has custody of the child.

- If the person committing the act is a teacher, school administrator, student teacher, school safety officer, or coach at the school the victim attends, age is not a factor.
  - If the act is committed by any other school personnel at the school the child attends, the offense occurs only if that person is at least four years older than the student.
- Crime against nature (G.S. 14-177). This common law offense is not further defined by statute. Courts have described it as sexual intercourse that is "contrary to the order of nature" and have held that it includes acts such as fellatio, sodomy, and buggery.[60]
- Incest (G.S. 14-178). This offense occurs if intercourse takes place between a child and a parent, grandparent, step-parent, brother or sister (whether whole or half blood), or aunt or uncle. Age is a factor with respect to punishment but does not affect whether the offense occurred.
- Preparation of obscene photographs, slides, or motion pictures of the juvenile (G.S. 14-190.5).
- Employing or permitting the juvenile to assist in a violation of the obscenity laws (G.S. 14-190.6). The offense occurs only if the person committing the act is at least eighteen and the child is younger than sixteen.
- Dissemination of obscene material to a minor younger than sixteen (G.S. 14-190.7). The offense occurs only if the person committing the act is at least eighteen and the minor is younger than sixteen.
- Dissemination of obscene material to a minor younger than thirteen (G.S. 14-190.8). The offense occurs only if the person committing the act is at least eighteen and the minor is younger than thirteen.
- Displaying material harmful to minors at a commercial establishment (G.S. 14-190.14).
- Disseminating material harmful to minors or exhibiting a performance harmful to minors (G.S. 14-190.15). It is a defense if the person committing the act is the minor's parent or legal guardian or if the minor's parent or legal guardian consents.
- First-degree sexual exploitation of a minor (G.S. 14-190.16).
- Second-degree sexual exploitation of a minor (G.S. 14-190.17).
- Promoting the prostitution of a child (G.S. 14-205.3(b)).

- Taking indecent liberties with a child (G.S. 14-202.1). This offense occurs only if the person committing the act is at least sixteen and is at least five years older than the child and the child is younger than sixteen.[61]

In 2012, the General Assembly added to this list the new offense of unlawfully selling, surrendering, or purchasing a child (G.S. 14-43.14) and provided that a child whose parent, guardian, or custodian has sold or attempted to sell a child in violation of the statute is an abused juvenile for purposes of the Juvenile Code.[62]

In 2013, the General Assembly added three additional offenses: human trafficking (G.S. 14-43.11), involuntary servitude (G.S. 14-43.12), and sexual servitude (G.S. 14-43.13).[63]

Some of these offenses involve the use of force. Even when they do not, the acts covered by these offenses constitute criminal offenses even if the child apparently consents or participates in them voluntarily.

In determining whether a child's situation gives a person cause to suspect that the child is sexually abused, it helps to be familiar with this list. However, a person need not master or research the intricacies of criminal law. If inappropriate sexual conduct involving a child does not constitute one of these criminal offenses, the child still may be an abused or neglected juvenile and a report may be required based on other parts of the definitions.

Emotional Abuse

A child is *emotionally abused* if the child's parent, guardian, custodian, or caretaker creates—or allows others to create—serious emotional damage to the child. Evidence of serious emotional damage may include a child's "severe anxiety, depression, withdrawal, or aggressive behavior toward himself or herself or others."[64] This description is not always easy to apply, and few cases go to court solely on the basis of emotional abuse. In one case that involved both neglect and emotional abuse, the court found that the children had suffered serious emotional damage as a result of the parents' longstanding and acrimonious marital disputes.[65] In another, the court found that the mother's emotionally abusive conduct included force-feeding the child, humiliating him by displaying his wet pants to his classmates after he wet himself at school, and subjecting him to verbal abuse, bullying, and intimidation.[66]

Obviously, serious emotional damage is not always caused by emotional abuse, and children may suffer from depression or anxiety or be aggressive for a variety of reasons. Because causation is so hard to prove, many cases of emotional abuse probably are treated as neglect. A parent who creates or allows serious emotional damage to a child most likely is not providing the child with proper care, supervision, or discipline, so that the child is a neglected juvenile. A person deciding whether to make a report does not need to be concerned about whether the child's condition is more appropriately characterized as abused or neglected.

Contributing to Delinquency

Finally, a child is considered to be abused, for purposes of the reporting law, if the child's parent, guardian, custodian, or caretaker "encourages, directs, or approves" of the child's commission of delinquent acts involving moral turpitude.[67] In North Carolina a "delinquent act" is conduct by a juvenile who is at least six but not yet sixteen that would be a crime if committed by an adult.[68] Among the crimes that courts have said involve moral turpitude are conspiracy to possess with intent to distribute marijuana;[69] burglary;[70] and common law robbery, felonious larceny, and credit card fraud.[71]

Dependency

A juvenile is "dependent," for purposes of the reporting law, if the child needs assistance or placement because

1. no parent, guardian, or custodian is responsible for the child's care or supervision; or
2. the child's parent, guardian, or custodian is not able to provide for the child's care or supervision and does not have an appropriate alternative child care arrangement.[72]

Dependency results from a parent's inability to provide for the child more often than from the child's having no parent, guardian, or custodian to be responsible for the child's care. The cause of the parent's inability to care for the child is not important.[73] A parent's inability might be due to the parent's physical or mental illness or disability, an injury, the parent's arrest, or a natural disaster, and it may be temporary or permanent.

A parent also might be unable to provide for a child because of the child's own conduct or the child's extraordinary needs.[74] A child's severe illness or disability may place such demands on the parents that their best efforts are not sufficient to provide adequate care for the child or for both that child and other children in the home. Even when parents are not able to care for their children, for whatever reason, the responsibility for developing an alternative plan of care falls first on the parents themselves. The child is dependent only if the parent who is not able to care for his or her child has no alternate plan for the child's care or if the parent's plan is inappropriate or inadequate. A child might be dependent, for example, if her single parent had to undergo major surgery and no one else was available to care for the child in her absence. If the hospitalized parent had arranged for the child to stay temporarily with a responsible relative, however, the child would not be dependent despite the parent's inability to care for the child.

If a parent who cannot care for a child has the ability to make appropriate alternative arrangements but fails to do so, the line between dependency and neglect can blur. For example, if the hospitalized parent left an eight-year-old child at home with instructions to take care of herself for a week, the child probably would be neglected rather than dependent, or she might be both. For the person considering whether to make a report, it does not matter whether dependent or neglected is the more appropriate characterization of the child's condition. If the person has cause to suspect that a child's condition falls within either definition, the law requires that person to make a report to social services.

Maltreatment

Any person or institution with cause to suspect that a child has died as the result of maltreatment must report the case of that child to the county department of social services.[75] The Juvenile Code does not define *maltreatment*. When a child's death is the result of suspected abuse or neglect, as the Code defines those terms, the law almost certainly requires a report to social services. Maltreatment, though, appears to be a broader term, since the legislature easily could have said "children who die as the result of suspected abuse or neglect." Maltreatment might include, for example, action by someone other than a child's parent, guardian, custodian, or caretaker that results in the child's death.

Interpreting maltreatment as being broader than abuse and neglect is consistent with the General Assembly's creation of a child fatality prevention system that includes the North Carolina Child Fatality Task Force, state and local Child Fatality Prevention Teams, and county Community Child Protection Teams.[76] This system provides for multidisciplinary state and local teams to review all deaths of children under age eighteen in North Carolina, with one purpose being to identify any deficiencies in the delivery of public services that are designed to prevent child abuse, neglect, or death.[77]

A county social services department's immediate response to a report of a child's death due to maltreatment focuses on determining whether other children remain in the home (or the institutional setting) and, if they do, determining whether those children require protective services or need to be removed for their protection.[78]

Difficulty in Applying the Definitions—An Example

Obviously, terms like "proper care," "necessary medical care," "substantial risk," and "injurious environment" lend themselves to varying interpretations. Questions framed in terms of whether particular facts are covered by these or other terms often do not yield the unequivocal answers that people want. Some frequently asked questions about applying the definitions are discussed in Chapter 14, "Schools and School Personnel," and Chapter 15, "Health and Mental Health Professionals and Facilities."[79] The question discussed below illustrates the kind of quandary someone who wants to comply with the reporting law might face.

Does the fact that a minor female is living with or regularly having sexual intercourse with her older boyfriend mean that she is abused, neglected, or dependent?

A minor (someone under age eighteen) who leaves home, with or without parental consent, is not emancipated unless the minor marries or obtains a court order of emancipation. The minor's parents remain legally responsible for the minor's care and supervision,[80] and the reporting law continues to apply. This remains true even if the minor becomes pregnant, gives birth to a child, or fathers a child.

If the girl is thirteen, fourteen, or fifteen years old and the boyfriend is at least four years older than she is, the boyfriend's engaging in intercourse or sexual acts with her is statutory rape or statutory sexual offense.[81] This is true even if the relationship is totally voluntary on the girl's part. No law requires that these crimes be reported to law enforcement. The offenses of statutory rape and statutory sexual offense against thirteen-, fourteen-, and fifteen-year-olds were added to the criminal laws in 1995. The part of the Juvenile Code definition of "abused juvenile" that references a variety of criminal sex offenses has never been amended to include these offenses. Thus, the Code does not explicitly provide that a juvenile is abused if a parent, guardian, custodian, or caretaker permits or encourages the commission of statutory rape or statutory sexual offense against a child who is thirteen, fourteen, or fifteen years of age. Nevertheless, a report in that circumstance almost certainly would be required on the basis that the parent is not providing proper care and supervision and that the girl is therefore neglected. Even if the parent is not committing, permitting, or encouraging the conduct, a report may be required on the basis that the parent is not providing or is not able to provide proper care and supervision for the child.

Any time a report to a social services department involves allegations of a crime committed against a child, the department must notify law enforcement and the district attorney if the report indicates that the child "may have been physically harmed . . . by [a] person other than the juvenile's parent, guardian, custodian, or caretaker."[82] The law does not provide guidance as to what constitutes *physical harm* for purposes of that requirement.

When sexual activity occurs and the girl is sixteen or seventeen years old, or any time the boyfriend is not four or more years older than the girl, none of the criminal sex offense statutes apply if the conduct is consensual. Still, the girl—and the boy if he is younger than eighteen—may be neglected or dependent if the parents are not providing or are not able to provide the minor with proper care and supervision. By itself, consensual sexual activity between older teens—although it may cause family, social, medical, or other concerns—usually is not an appropriate basis for a report to social services. Each situation should be assessed in terms of likely harm or risk of harm to the minor and the purposes of the reporting law.

In cases in which a minor's parents do not condone the minor's living arrangement or conduct and have made real but unsuccessful efforts to get the minor to return home or stop seeing a boyfriend or girlfriend, the minor might be considered an undisciplined juvenile. There is no reporting requirement related to this category of juveniles, which includes a juvenile who "is regularly disobedient to and beyond the disciplinary control of the juvenile's parent, guardian, or custodian; or . . . has run away from home for a period of more than 24 hours."[83] In that case, the parents could seek help from juvenile court counselors in the local Juvenile Justice office.[84] In the case of a runaway who has been away from home for more than twenty-four hours, a law enforcement officer is authorized to take the juvenile into custody and release the juvenile to the parents.[85]

Other questions that have similarly imprecise answers and that require case by case analysis include the following:

- Should the fact that a twelve-year-old girl is pregnant or has a venereal disease always create "cause to suspect" that she is abused or neglected and require a report? What if the girl is thirteen? Or fifteen? Or seventeen? Or ten?
- Is a parent's insistence on using only alternative medicine in response to a child's medical needs ever neglect that must be reported?[86]
- When does knowing that a child has witnessed domestic violence or that the child lives in a home where domestic violence occurs require a report?[87]

Sometimes the answers become clear with the addition of other relevant information. In some cases additional guidance may come from legislative changes, appellate court decisions, or state social services policy. For social services departments and courts, these and other questions require careful individual assessment in light of available information and the purposes of the child protective services system. On a broader scale, they require local collaboration to find the best ways to direct appropriate information and services to the affected families and children.

Someone deciding whether to make a report also should carefully assess all available information and consider the purposes of the reporting law and child protective services system. Rather than feeling stymied by the kinds of uncertainty described above, however, he or she should keep in mind that the threshold for reporting is "cause to suspect" and that the social services department will screen out a report it determines was not required.

Notes

1. North Carolina General Statutes (hereinafter G.S.) § 7B-301. The North Carolina General Statutes can be viewed online at www.ncga.state.nc.us/gascripts/Statutes/StatutesTOC.pl.

2. G.S. 7B-805.

3. G.S. 7B-101(15).

4. *See, e.g., In re* Moore, 306 N.C. 394, 293 S.E.2d 127 (1982), *appeal dismissed,* 459 U.S. 1139 (1983); *In re* Clark, 303 N.C. 592, 281 S.E.2d 47 (1981); *In re* Allen, 58 N.C. App. 322, 293 S.E.2d 607 (1982); *In re* Huber, 57 N.C. App. 453, 291 S.E.2d 916, *appeal dismissed and review denied,* 306 N.C. 557, 294 S.E.2d 223 (1982).

5. *In re* Biggers, 50 N.C. App. 332, 341, 274 S.E.2d 236, 241 (1981).

6. Unless a different meaning is clear from the context, the term "parent" should be read to include guardian, custodian, or caretaker in this discussion of the definitions.

7. *In re* Cusson, 43 N.C. App. 333, 258 S.E.2d 858 (1979).

8. *In re* Devone, 86 N.C. App. 57, 356 S.E.2d 389 (1987); *In re* McMillan, 30 N.C. App. 235, 226 S.E.2d 693 (1976). See the section below entitled "Difficulty in Applying the Definitions—An Example."

9. Home schooling in North Carolina is overseen by the North Carolina Division of Non-Public Education (DNPE) in the state Department of Administration. Complaints about a home school that is registered with DNPE should be made to that division. Concerns about a home school that is not registered should be directed to local school officials. The procedures for home-school complaints and a home-school citizen complaint form are available at www.ncdnpe.org/cc125.aspx and www.ncdnpe.org/documents/cc126.pdf.

10. Several criminal laws do specify particular ages in relation to the proper supervision of children. For example, G.S. 14-318 makes it a misdemeanor for any person to leave a child under the age of eight "locked or otherwise confined in any dwelling, building or enclosure, and go away from such dwelling, building or enclosure without leaving some person of the age of discretion in charge of the same, so as to expose the child to danger by fire." Under G.S. 14-316, it is a misdemeanor for a parent (or others in parent-like positions) to permit a child under the age of twelve to possess or use a dangerous firearm, regardless of whether it is loaded, except under the supervision of that adult.

11. See, for example, *In re W.V.,* 204 N.C. App. 290, 293, 693 S.E.2d 383, 386 (2010), quoting the following statement from *In re Safriet,* 112 N.C. App. 747, 752, 436 S.E.2d 898, 901–02 (1993): "[T]his Court has consistently required that there be some physical, mental, or emotional impairment of the juvenile or a substantial risk of such impairment as a consequence of the failure to provide 'proper care, supervision, or discipline.'" *See also In re* D.B.J., 197 N.C. App. 752, 678 S.E.2d 778 (2009) (affirming a neglect adjudication based on a substantial risk to the child based on the parents' abuse and neglect of another child in the home, domestic violence, and substance abuse).

12. *See, e.g.,* Powers v. Powers, 130 N.C. App. 37, 502 S.E.2d 398 (affirming a neglect adjudication where evidence showed not only that the mother had a serious problem with alcohol but also that she drove with the children in the car while intoxicated,

she had become so intoxicated at home that she was unable to care for the children, and her alcohol problem contributed to the children's emotional problems), *review denied*, 349 N.C. 530, 526 S.E.2d 180 (1998).

13. G.S. 7B-101(1).

14. *In re* Thompson, 64 N.C. App. 95, 100, 306 S.E.2d 792, 795 (1983).

15. *In re* A.J.M., 177 N.C. App. 745, 751, 630 S.E.2d 33, 36 (2006).

16. *In re* Mashburn, 162 N.C. App. 386, 591 S.E.2d 584 (2004).

17. *In re* Kennedy, 103 N.C. App. 632, 406 S.E.2d 307 (1991).

18. *Thompson*, 64 N.C. App. at 99, 306 S.E.2d at 794.

19. See U.S. Department of Health & Human Services, Administration for Children & Families, Child Welfare Information Gateway, "Discipline Versus Abuse," identifying resources related to the difference between physical discipline and physical abuse and to cultural contexts and ethnic differences relating to discipline, www.childwelfare.gov/can/defining/disc_abuse.cfm.

20. *See* Pratt v. Bishop, 257 N.C. 486, 126 S.E.2d 597 (1962); *In re* Adoption of Searle, 82 N.C. App. 273, 346 S.E.2d 511 (1986).

21. *See* G.S. 7B-1111(a)(7). *See also In re* Young, 346 N.C. 244, 485 S.E.2d 612 (1997) (holding that evidence of willfulness was insufficient to establish abandonment); *In re* M.D., 200 N.C. App. 35, 682 S.E.2d 780 (2009) (affirming termination of parental rights on grounds of abandonment where father visited one daughter only once in three years and had not seen his other daughter for more than three years); *In re* Graham, 63 N.C. App. 146, 303 S.E.2d 624 (holding that lack of involvement with children for more than two years established a pattern of abandonment and neglect), *review denied*, 309 N.C. 320, 307 S.E.2d 170 (1983); *In re* Apa, 59 N.C. App. 322, 296 S.E.2d 811 (1982) (holding that a father's willful failure to support or visit his child for a period of eleven years constituted abandonment and neglect).

22. G.S. 7B-302(a).

23. *Id.*

24. *See* G.S. 14-318.2(c), -318.4(c), and -322.3. The legislation, S.L. 2001-291, became effective July 19, 2001. For a more thorough discussion of this law, see Janet Mason, "Legal Abandonment of Newborns: North Carolina's Safe Surrender Law," *Popular Government* 75 (Fall 2009): 29–36, http://sogpubs.unc.edu/electronicversions/pg/pgfal09/article5.pdf.

25. *See* G.S. 7B-500.

26. *In re* Hayden, 96 N.C. App. 77, 384 S.E.2d 558 (1989).

27. *In re* S.W., 187 N.C. App. 505, 653 S.E.2d 425 (2007). *See also In re* C.M., 183 N.C. App. 207, 644 S.E.2d 588 (2007) (affirming a neglect adjudication where evidence showed, among other things, that the child's father delayed seeking medical attention for the child despite having been encouraged by a social worker to do so); *In re* C.P., 181 N.C. App. 698, 641 S.E.2d 13 (2007) (affirming a neglect adjudication where the mother delayed seeking necessary medical care for the child for his bruising and his disciplinary, behavioral, and developmental problems).

28. *In re* Huber, 57 N.C. App. 453, 291 S.E.2d 916, *appeal dismissed and review denied*, 306 N.C. 557, 294 S.E.2d 223 (1982).

29. *Id.* at 458, 291 S.E.2d at 919.

30. U.S. Department of Health & Human Services, Child Welfare Information Gateway, "Definitions of Child Abuse and Neglect" (current through Feb. 2011), www.childwelfare.gov/systemwide/laws_policies/statutes/define.pdf#Page=1&view=Fit. The federal Child Abuse Prevention and Treatment Act makes clear that it does not establish a federal requirement that a parent provide a child with medical services or treatment that is against the parent's religious beliefs. *See* 42 U.S.C. § 5106i(a)(1).

31. *In re* Stratton, 153 N.C. App. 428, 433, 571 S.E.2d 234, 237 (2002) (citations omitted). G.S. 130A-157 provides an exemption from the immunization requirements based on a parent's bona fide religious beliefs. The issue in *Stratton* was whether the parents lost their right to claim that exemption when the children were adjudicated neglected and removed from their custody.

32. *In re* Browning, 124 N.C. App. 190, 193–94, 476 S.E.2d 465, 467 (2002) (citations omitted).

33. *In re* N.F., 194 N.C. App. 820, 671 S.E.2d 599 (2009) (unpublished).

34. *In re* Greene, 152 N.C. App. 410, 417, 568 S.E.2d 634, 638 (2002).

35. *In re* McCabe, 157 N.C. App. 673, 674–76, 580 S.E.2d 69, 70–71 (2003). Doctors in this case had diagnosed Munchausen syndrome by proxy, which involves a parent's causing real or apparent indications of illness in a child, and the opinion discusses the medical evidence.

36. *In re* Morales, 159 N.C. App. 429, 583 S.E.2d 692 (2003).

37. *See In re* Evans, 81 N.C. App. 449, 344 S.E.2d 325 (1986); *In re* Adcock, 69 N.C. App. 222, 316 S.E.2d 347 (1984) (holding that moving eight times within a year and a half was evidence of instability relevant to a neglect determination).

38. *In re* Helms, 127 N.C. App. 505, 491 S.E.2d 672 (1997).

39. *See, e.g., In re* W.V., 204 N.C. App. 290, 294, 693 S.E.2d 383, 386–87 (2010) (citing, among other things, the fact that the parent engaged in domestic violence in the child's presence); *In re* C.M., 198 N.C. App. 53, 678 S.E.2d 794 (2009) (stating that the environment in which the children lived was injurious because it involved violence).

40. *In re* K.W., 192 N.C. App. 646, 666 S.E.2d 490 (2008).

41. *See, e.g., W.V.*, 204 N.C. App. at 294, 693 S.E.2d at 387 (citing, among other things, the fact that the parent grew and consumed an illegal controlled substance in the home).

42. Powers v. Powers, 130 N.C. App. 37, 502 S.E.2d 398, *review denied*, 349 N.C. 530, 526 S.E.2d 180 (1998).

43. *Id.* at 43, 502 S.E.2d at 402.

44. *See* G.S. Chapter 131D, Article 1A. Unless specifically exempted, a person or agency that violates these requirements is guilty of a misdemeanor.

45. G.S. 48-3-201. Placement of a child for adoption by anyone else is a Class 1 misdemeanor. G.S. 48-10-101(c).

46. G.S. 7B-3800 through -3806.

47. G.S. 48-10-102, -103.

48. G.S. 14-43.11(a); *see generally* G.S. 14-43.10 through -43.13.

49. *See* Jeff Welty, "Is It a Crime to Sell a Baby?" *North Carolina Criminal Law: UNC School of Government* (blog), April 26, 2010, http://sogweb.sog.unc.edu/blogs/ncclaw/?p=1232.

50. S.L. 2012-153 created the new offense, a Class F felony, in G.S. 14-43.14, which became effective December 1, 2012.

51. G.S. 14-43.14.

52. *See In re* M.G., 363 N.C. 570, 573–74, 681 S.E.2d 290, 292 (2009).

53. *Id.* at 574, 681 S.E.2d at 292. Clearly the court was giving the term "caretaker" a broader meaning than the one found in the Juvenile Code's definition of that term.

54. G.S. 7B-101(1).

55. G.S. 14-318.4(d)(2). The statute distinguishes between "serious physical injury" and "serious bodily injury." The latter, which is required for a conviction of the more serious offense of Class B2 felony child abuse, is defined as an "injury that creates a substantial risk of death or that causes serious permanent disfigurement, coma, a permanent or protracted condition that causes extreme pain, or permanent or protracted loss or impairment of the function of any bodily member or organ, or that results in prolonged hospitalization." G.S. 14-318.4(d)(1).

56. *In re* L.T.R., 181 N.C. App. 376, 639 S.E.2d 122 (2007).

57. *See, e.g., In re* C.B., 180 N.C. App. 221, 221–22, 636 S.E.2d 336, 337 (2006) (holding that where the only evidence of abuse in the record was the father's spanking or whipping of the child with a belt, resulting in a bruise on the child's buttocks, the evidence did not support a finding of "serious injury" or an adjudication that the child was abused), *aff'd per curiam*, 361 N.C. 345, 643 S.E.2d 587 (2007).

58. *In re* K.A., ___ N.C. App. ___, 720 S.E.2d 461 (2011) (unpublished).

59. *See, e.g.*, State v. Paddock, 204 N.C. App. 280, 287, 696 S.E.2d 529, 534 (2010) (affirming convictions of first-degree murder and felonious child abuse inflicting serious bodily injury and finding no error in the admission of expert testimony that a child "was the victim of ritualistic child abuse, sadistic child abuse, and torture"), *review denied*, 364 N.C. 330, 701 S.E.2d 251.

60. *See, e.g., In re* R.L.C., 361 N.C. 287, 643 S.E.2d 920 (2007); State v. Harward, 264 N.C. 746, 142 S.E.2d 691 (1965).

61. The statutes defining the criminal offenses listed here can be accessed at www.ncga.state.nc.us/gascripts/Statutes/StatutesTOC.pl?Chapter=0014.

62. S.L. 2012-153 created this statute, which applies only to offenses committed on or after December 1, 2012.

63. S.L. 2013-368, sec. 16, which made these additions, applies to offenses committed on or after October 1, 2013.

64. G.S. 7B-101(1)e.

65. Powers v. Powers, 130 N.C. App. 37, 502 S.E.2d 398, *review denied*, 349 N.C. 530, 526 S.E.2d 180 (1998).

66. *In re* J.H-S., ___ N.C. App. ___, 714 S.E.2d 866 (2011) (unpublished).

67. G.S. 7B-101(1)f. The North Carolina Supreme Court has referred to "moral turpitude" as involving "an act of inherent baseness in the private, social, or public duties which one owes to his fellowmen or to society, or to his country, her institutions and her government." State v. Mann, 317 N.C. 164, 170, 345 S.E.2d 365, 369 (1986) (internal quotation marks, citations omitted).

68. G.S. 7B-1501(7). In North Carolina, a sixteen- or seventeen-year-old is treated as an adult for purposes of his or her criminal behavior. A sixteen-year-old whose parent encouraged him or her to steal, therefore, probably is not covered by this part of the abuse definition because a sixteen-year-old does not commit delinquent acts—he

or she commits crimes. Still, the sixteen-year-old could be considered neglected because the parent is failing to provide proper supervision and discipline. Or a court might determine that the context and purpose of the statute indicate a legislative intent to include criminal conduct by sixteen- and seventeen-year-old juveniles as well as delinquent conduct by younger children.

69. Dew v. State *ex rel.* N.C. Dep't of Motor Vehicles, 127 N.C. App. 309, 488 S.E.2d 836 (1997).

70. State v. Collins, 334 N.C. 54, 431 S.E.2d 188 (1993).

71. State v. Shelly, 176 N.C. App. 575, 584, 627 S.E.2d 287, 295 (2006).

72. G.S. 7B-101(9).

73. Older cases may reflect the pre-1997 wording of the statute, which required that the parent, guardian, or custodian's inability to care for the child be "due to physical or mental incapacity." See S.L. 1997-113.

74. While such children are not necessarily excluded from the definition of "dependent juvenile," their needs generally can be addressed more appropriately through systems other than child protective services, such as mental health, developmental disabilities, and substance abuse services; juvenile justice and delinquency prevention services; or other community resources.

75. G.S. 7B-301.

76. *See* G.S. 7B-1400 *et seq.*

77. G.S. 7B-1400.

78. G.S. 7B-302(b).

79. See Chapter 11 for a related discussion of screening—the process by which social services departments decide whether to accept reports for assessment.

80. G.S. 7B-3400.

81. G.S. 14-27.7A. Offenses involving a minor who is under the age of thirteen are described in G.S. 14-27.2, -27.2A(a), -27.4, and -27.4A(a). Each of these offenses (but not G.S. 14-27.7A) is listed in the definition of "abused juvenile" in G.S. 7B-101(1)d. and requires a report to social services if the offense is committed, encouraged, or allowed by the minor's parent, guardian, custodian, or caretaker.

82. *See* G.S. 7B-307(a).

83. G.S. 7B-1501(27).

84. *See* G.S. Chapter 7B, Article 17 (Screening of Delinquency and Undisciplined Complaints).

85. G.S. 7B-1900, -1901. A rarely used statute authorizes a parent to file a civil action in district court asking the court to order a minor to return home and to order another person not to harbor the juvenile or allow the juvenile to remain in that person's home or on that person's premises. *See* G.S. 7B-3404. The status of that law is unclear, however. In 1998, the court of appeals held that it applied only with respect to sixteen- and seventeen-year-olds, who at that time were not included in the definition of "undisciplined juvenile." With respect to other juveniles, the court said, the Juvenile Code provisions relating to undisciplined juveniles are exclusive. *See* Taylor v. Robinson, 131 N.C. App. 337, 508 S.E.2d 289 (1998). Subsequently the definition of undisciplined juvenile was amended to include sixteen- and seventeen-year-olds.

86. *See* Kavitha V. Neerukonda, J.D., M.H.A., "Choosing Alternative Treatments for Children," *American Medical Association Journal of Ethics, Virtual Mentor* 13, no. 6 (June 2011): 369–73, http://virtualmentor.ama-assn.org/2011/06/hlaw1-1106.html.

87. *See In re* A.N.L., ___ N.C. App. ___, 714 S.E.2d 189 (2011) (affirming an order adjudicating an infant to be abused and neglected based on evidence that a physical altercation occurred between the parents while the mother was holding the infant). State social services policies relating to domestic violence and child protective services can be found at http://info.dhhs.state.nc.us/olm/manuals/dss/csm-60/man/CS1409.htm#TopOfPage.

Part 3. Responsibilities and Rights of Reporters

Chapter 6

Who Must Report

General Rule

North Carolina's reporting law applies to every person and every institution in the state. It requires "[a]ny person or institution who has cause to suspect that any juvenile is abused, neglected, or dependent, as defined by G.S. 7B-101, or has died as the result of maltreatment" to make a report to the county department of social services.[1] The reporting requirement applies to doctors, social workers, therapists, teachers, law enforcement officers, and others whose professions sometimes involve them directly with problems of abuse, neglect, or dependency. It applies equally, though, to housing inspectors, store clerks, coworkers, friends, relatives, bystanders, and everyone else.

When the person considering making a report has a personal or professional relationship with the child or the child's family, that person may want to discuss the perceived problem with the family. That relationship, however, should not be considered grounds for delaying a report. Of course, the reporting law does not permit anyone—professional, friend, or relative—to make an agreement not to report in exchange for an assurance that the person who may be responsible for a child's being abused, neglected, or dependent will seek help or take other actions.

Confidential and Privileged Communications

With one very small exception for attorneys, which is discussed below, North Carolina law provides that "[n]o privilege shall be grounds for any person or institution failing to report that a juvenile may have been abused, neglected, or dependent, even if the knowledge or suspicion is acquired in an official professional capacity."[2] One of the main reasons reporting laws were first enacted, after all, was to allow, encourage, or require physicians to make reports despite the physician–patient privilege and the principle of medical confidentiality.[3]

Attorneys

The Juvenile Code (the Code) contains only one exception to the otherwise universal duty to report. An attorney is not required to make a report if the knowledge or suspicion that otherwise would require a report comes from a client the attorney is representing in an abuse, neglect, or dependency case.[4] In any other situation, the law requires attorneys to report the same as everyone else. If an attorney learns from a parent about that parent's abuse or neglect of a child, or about the parent's inability to care adequately for the child, while representing the parent in a child support action, a divorce, or any other matter that does not involve the abuse, neglect, or dependency itself, no statutory exception excludes the attorney from the duty to report.

This legal duty may conflict with a lawyer's ethical obligation to maintain the confidentiality of client information.[5] The North Carolina State Bar, which adopts and interprets Rules of Professional Conduct for the legal profession, concluded that for purposes of complying with those rules, lawyers have broad discretion in deciding how to resolve the conflict. In a 1995 ethics opinion interpreting its rules in relation to the child abuse and neglect reporting law, the State Bar concluded that a lawyer ethically could report suspected abuse or neglect to social services, in compliance with the reporting law, even if the report might result in substantial harm to the client's interests.[6] The opinion also stated, however, that a lawyer ethically could decide not to make a report if the report would "substantially undermine the purpose of the representation or substantially damage" the client's interests. A lawyer deciding not to make a report in that circumstance would be in violation of the reporting law but not of the Rules of Professional Conduct.

An attorney weighing compliance with the reporting law and preservation of the confidentiality of client information should consider, among other things, whether making a report would deprive his or her client of a constitutional right—such as the right to effective assistance of counsel in a criminal case.[7] When the two are inconsistent, a client's federal constitutional right would supersede an attorney's duty under state law to report child abuse, neglect, or dependency.[8]

Judges

Like everyone else in North Carolina, any judge who has cause to suspect that a child is abused, neglected, or dependent must make a report to the county department of social services. A report would be required, for example, if credible evidence in a child custody case gave the judge cause to suspect that one or both of the parties had disciplined their child in a cruel and harmful way. Domestic violence cases may generate occasions for reporting. They also present a challenge for judges and others who must decide whether information about a child's home situation (1) creates cause to suspect that the child is abused, neglected, or dependent or (2) indicates less than ideal circumstances but does not rise to a level of concern that warrants an assessment by the department of social services. That determination must be made with reference to the safety and well-being of the child, not just the conduct of the parents.

Occasionally a judge hearing a custody dispute between parents will conclude that neither parent is fit to have custody of the child. Although the court in that situation probably has authority to place the child directly in the custody of the department of social services,[9] a report to the department of social services pursuant to the Juvenile Code is more appropriate, given the extensive statutory scheme the Code provides for responding to children who are abused, neglected, or dependent. If the court makes a report to social services and the department determines that the child is abused, neglected, or dependent, it can file a juvenile petition and, if necessary, take immediate custody of the child before filing a petition and obtaining a custody order in the juvenile proceeding.[10] If the court places the child directly in the department's custody in the civil action, the child is not entitled to a guardian ad litem as in a juvenile case (pursuant to G.S. 7B-601); the parent is not entitled to appointed counsel if indigent; and federal funds probably will not cover the cost of the child's foster care placement. In addition, if social services is given custody in a civil action and its assessment does not substantiate abuse, neglect, or dependency, the department is left in the awkward position of having custody of a child and being party to a civil custody action with no statutory guidance as to how it should proceed.

The court in a civil custody action does not have jurisdiction to adjudicate a child to be abused, neglected, or dependent—that jurisdiction exists exclusively in a juvenile court proceeding.[11] Neither does the court have jurisdiction to initiate a juvenile proceeding on its own motion or to order social services to assume "nonsecure custody" of a child under the Juvenile Code when the department has not filed a petition alleging that the child is abused, neglected, or dependent.[12] There is no statutory authority for a judge to order a social services department to conduct an assessment or investigation to determine whether a child is abused, neglected, or dependent. Instead, the court should make a report of suspected abuse, neglect, or dependency to the department, which would then follow its statutory obligations and procedures for responding to reports.[13]

A judge may learn of (or develop cause to suspect) abuse, neglect, or dependency during a court proceeding that is required to be strictly confidential. The United States Supreme Court has held that a state may not constitutionally require parental consent for a minor to obtain an abortion unless the state also provides a confidential judicial procedure through which the minor can seek a waiver of the parental consent requirement.[14] North Carolina's waiver (also called judicial bypass) statute requires that the court proceeding, records relating to it, and the pregnant minor's identity be kept strictly confidential.[15] The statute also provides, however, that a judge who finds that the minor has been a victim of incest must notify the director of the department of social services "for further action" pursuant to the Juvenile Code provisions relating to abuse and neglect.[16] Contacting a juvenile's parents is part of every assessment a social services department conducts in response to a report.

North Carolina courts have not examined the degree to which a report of incest might interfere with the minor's right to confidentiality or whether the much broader reporting requirement in the Juvenile Code ever applies with respect to information a judge obtains in a judicial bypass proceeding.[17] The Fourth Circuit Court of Appeals, however, characterized as "unconscionable" the proposition that judges cannot be required to report abuse they learn about in judicial bypass proceedings. The court said:

> Appellants would have a judge, who is sworn to uphold the law, withhold vital information regarding rape or incest which would allow

state authorities to end the abuse, protect the victim, and punish the abuser. Not only would Appellants' position prevent the judge from helping the victim seeking the abortion, but it would prevent the judge from helping other juveniles in the same household under the same threat of incest. This Court does not believe that the Constitution requires judges to be placed in such an untenable position.[18]

The opinion suggests that the court would apply the same reasoning not only to the specific duty to report incest under the abortion consent waiver statute, but also to the duty under the Juvenile Code to report abuse, neglect, and dependency. The Fourth Circuit quoted with approval from a concurring opinion by Justice Kennedy in a U.S. Supreme Court case:

'No one can contend that a minor who is pregnant is somehow less deserving of the State's protection. It is reasonable to provide that any minor who contends that she cannot notify her parent or parents because she is the victim of neglect or abuse must allow the State to use its power to investigate her declaration and protect her from harm.'[19]

Religious Officials
Some states' reporting laws explicitly include clergy among the people who are mandated to report child abuse or neglect. In other states clergy are specifically exempted from the duty to report, at least to the extent that the information they have derives from "pastoral communications."[20] North Carolina's statute does not address religious officials and the duty to report. Therefore, they apparently are included in the mandate that "any person" with cause to suspect child abuse, neglect, or dependency must make a report to the department of social services.[21] A religious official, like everyone else, has a duty to report regardless of that official's relationship to the child. Whether mistreatment of a child by a religious official is abuse or neglect that must be reported to the social services department depends on whether that religious official is the child's parent, guardian, custodian, or caretaker. (The definition of "caretaker" is discussed in Chapter 4.)

North Carolina law relating to the competence of witnesses to testify in court has long recognized a clergy–communicant privilege.[22] Unlike most other statutory privileges, the clergy–communicant privilege statute includes neither an exception for child abuse and neglect cases nor authority for the court to compel disclosure upon finding that disclosure is necessary to a proper administration of justice.[23] Before July 1, 1999, the Juvenile Code explicitly overrode certain specified privileges, including husband–wife and doctor–patient but not the clergy–communicant privilege. Since that time, however, the Code has provided unequivocally that no privilege, except a narrow attorney–client privilege, is grounds for failing to report suspected abuse, neglect, or dependency or for excluding evidence in a case involving the abuse, neglect, or dependency of a child.[24]

Confidential communications between a person and his or her rabbi, minister, priest, or other religious confidant might be viewed as part of that individual's exercise of his or her protected religious freedom. One can imagine a constitutional challenge to the application of the reporting requirement to clergy on that basis. On the other hand, a state's exempting the clergy privilege while abrogating the privileges involved when a person seeks similar counsel from a non-religious professional could form the basis for a different kind of challenge.[25]

Researchers

Like many clinicians and practitioners, researchers may find their professional objectives and ethics in conflict with a duty to report suspected child abuse, neglect, or dependency. Especially when the research itself concerns child abuse and neglect, obtaining informed consent from research participants may be hindered by disclosure of the researcher's legal duty to report suspected abuse or neglect.[26] On the other hand, without the disclosure, the participant's consent is not fully informed if he or she has been told that the information provided will be kept confidential. Even when the research is totally unrelated to abuse or neglect, information a researcher obtains may give that person cause to suspect that a child is abused or neglected.

State law provides no exception or exemption for researchers. Some researchers, however, may obtain a limited exemption under the following federal law authorizing the federal Secretary of Health and Human Services to issue Certificates of Confidentiality:

> The Secretary may authorize persons engaged in biomedical, behavioral, clinical, or other research (including research on mental health, including research on the use and effect of alcohol and other psychoactive drugs) to protect the privacy of individuals who are the subject of such research by withholding from all persons not connected with the

conduct of such research the names or other identifying characteristics of such individuals. Persons so authorized to protect the privacy of such individuals may not be compelled in any Federal, State, or local civil, criminal, administrative, legislative, or other proceedings to identify such individuals.[27]

The certificates are designed to protect researchers from being compelled to disclose information that would identify research participants, in order to promote participation in studies by assuring confidentiality. The Secretary of Health and Human Services has delegated authority to issue certificates to the National Institutes of Health (NIH), and applications for certificates go through NIH regardless of whether the research involves NIH funding.[28] A researcher may voluntarily disclose information that is protected by a certificate, including information relating to child abuse, if the informed consent form provides for such disclosures.[29]

Summary

Except for a very limited statutory exception for attorneys, possible constitutional exceptions, and Certificates of Confidentiality for researchers, the reporting law makes no accommodation for professionals who—because of tradition, ethics, or legal obligation—consider confidentiality an essential element of their relationships with clients or patients.

The reporting requirement can raise troublesome questions and issues for these professionals:

- When and how should school guidance counselors, physicians, psychologists, and others inform people who come to them for assistance that the law requires confidentiality to be broken if necessary to report suspected child abuse, neglect, or dependency?
- If students, patients, or clients are informed or reminded that suspected abuse, neglect, or dependency must be reported, will those who need help be discouraged from seeking it?

The tension between the reporting law and the need to encourage trust and disclosure in order to provide effective services is long-standing and ongoing. Affected professionals—both individually and collectively—struggle to resolve that tension and, no doubt, will continue to do so.

Periodically proposals are made to change the law to carve out more exceptions. Unless the law is changed, though, it requires reporting even by those who fear that a report may do more harm than good.

Notes

1. North Carolina General Statutes (hereinafter G.S.) § 7B-301. The North Carolina General Statutes can be viewed online at www.ncga.state.nc.us/gascripts/Statutes/StatutesTOC.pl.

2. *Id.* State mental health law provides specifically that mental health, developmental disability, and substance abuse facilities must disclose confidential information for purposes of complying with the child abuse, neglect, and dependency reporting law. G.S. 122C-54(h).

3. The terms "privilege" and "confidentiality," although sometimes used interchangeably, do not have exactly the same meaning. Privilege generally refers to a statutory rule allowing a person to prevent the disclosure in court of communications between that person and a specified professional. Confidentiality, on the other hand, refers to a broader prohibition or restriction on the disclosure of information. Most privileges are statutory, and in North Carolina law they are set out in Article 7 of G.S. Chapter 8. While confidentiality may be based on statute, often it is an ethical duty deriving from professional standards rather than from law. *See, e.g.,* Sultan v. State Bd. of Exam'rs of Practicing Psychologists, 121 N.C. App. 739, 746, 468 S.E.2d 443, 447 (1996) (distinguishing the psychologist–patient privilege and a psychologist's "general professional obligation to maintain the confidentiality of client information").

4. G.S. 7B-310.

5. Rule 1.6 of the Revised Rules of Professional Conduct of the North Carolina State Bar (RPC) imposes strict limits on a lawyer's ability to reveal information acquired from a client in a professional relationship. The rule can be accessed at www.ncbar.gov/rules/rpcsearch.asp.

6. North Carolina State Bar, RPC 175 (Jan. 13, 1995), *2012 Lawyer's Handbook* (Abridged), 10-61 to 10-62. *See also* RPC 120 (July 17, 1992), *2012 Lawyer's Handbook* at 10-41 to 10-42. The *Handbook* is available at www.ncbar.gov/handbook/2012%20Handbook.pdf.

7. *See* RPC 175, cited in full in note 6, above. An attorney would have no guarantee that a court or the State Bar would agree with the attorney's conclusion that making a report would jeopardize the client's constitutional rights.

8. Neither the attorney–client privilege nor a lawyer's duty to maintain the confidentiality of client information is statutory. One legal scholar has concluded that for the most part the attorney–client privilege is not constitutionally required and that it could be legislatively eliminated in contexts other than criminal prosecutions. Robert P. Mosteller, *Child Abuse Reporting Laws and Attorney–Client Confidences: The Reality and the Specter of Lawyer as Informant*, 42 DUKE L.J. 203, 271–72 (1992). *See also* Katharyn I. Christian, *Putting Legal Doctrines to the Test: The Inclusion of Attorneys as Mandatory Reporters of Child Abuse*, 32 J. LEGAL PROF. 215 (2008).

9. *See* Isaac v. Wells, 189 N.C. App. 210, 657 S.E.2d 445 (2008) (unpublished), in which the court of appeals affirmed the trial court's order placing children in the custody of social services in a civil custody action but remanded for additional findings of fact and for the trial court to enter an order making the social services department a party to the civil action. Although the trial court's order had indicated that it was "reactivating" a juvenile case involving the same children, the appellate court held that jurisdiction in the juvenile case had been terminated. *See also* Wilson v. Wilson, 269 N.C. 676, 153 S.E.2d 349 (1967) (affirming an order entered in a civil custody action temporarily placing children in the custody of the county department of public welfare).

10. G.S. 7B-500(a).

11. G.S. 7B-200(a).

12. *See In re* Ivey, 156 N.C. App. 398, 576 S.E.2d 386 (2003).

13. *See* Ky. Cabinet for Health & Family Servs. v. Garber, 340 S.W.3d 588 (Ky. App. May 6, 2011) (affirming writs of prohibition directed to two trial court judges who, in domestic violence actions, ordered state Child Protective Services to investigate possible neglect or abuse and holding that issuing the orders instead of reporting suspected abuse or neglect violated the separation of powers provision of the state constitution).

14. Belloti v. Baird, 443 U.S. 622, *reh'g denied*, 444 U.S. 887 (1979).

15. G.S. 90-21.8.

16. G.S. 90-21.8(f).

17. Although all states have child abuse reporting laws, few courts seem to have addressed this issue. State legislatures address it in a variety of ways in judicial waiver statutes. *See, e.g.*, Tex. Fam. Code § 33.009 (requiring the court or the minor's guardian ad litem or attorney ad litem to report specified sexual offenses to law enforcement, child protective services, or another appropriate agency based on information obtained during a confidential judicial waiver proceeding).

18. Manning v. Hunt, 119 F.3d 254, 273 (4th Cir. 1997). The court, affirming a judgment of the federal district court, held that the district court had not abused its discretion when it denied a motion for a preliminary injunction and refused to enjoin the enforcement of the state statute. Thus, the court's holding was not that the statute is constitutional but, rather, that the plaintiffs challenging the statute were not likely to prevail on the merits at a trial on that issue.

19. *Manning*, 119 F.3d at 273, *quoting* Hodgson v. Minnesota, 497 U.S. 417, 493–94, 110 S. Ct. 2926, 2967–68 (1990) (Kennedy, J., was joined by Rehnquist, C.J., White, J., and Scalia, J., in his concurrence).

20. For a chart showing each state's treatment of clergy as mandated reporters, see U.S. Department of Health & Human Services (hereinafter DHHS), Administration for Children & Families, Child Welfare Information Gateway, "Clergy as Mandatory Reporters of Child Abuse and Neglect," 2012, www.childwelfare.gov/systemwide/laws_policies/statutes/clergymandated.cfm.

21. North Carolina is in a minority of states that both mandate reporting by "any person" and deny or do not address the clergy–penitent privilege in child abuse cases. See the chart in the publication cited in full in note 20.

22. G.S. 8-53.2 reads as follows: "No priest, rabbi, accredited Christian Science practitioner, or a clergyman or ordained minister of an established church shall be competent to testify in any action, suit or proceeding concerning any information which was communicated to him and entrusted to him in his professional capacity, and necessary to enable him to discharge the functions of his office according to the usual course of his practice or discipline, wherein such person so communicating such information about himself or another is seeking spiritual counsel and advice relative to and growing out of the information so imparted, provided, however, that this section shall not apply where [the] communicant in open court waives the privilege conferred."

23. When first enacted in 1959, the statute did give the court that authority. In 1967, however, the General Assembly amended the statute to delete that provision. 1967 N.C. Sess. Laws ch. 794. Thereafter the state supreme court held that the amendment indicated "the General Assembly's intent to remove from the trial courts any discretion to compel disclosure when the clergy–communicant's privilege exists." State v. Barber, 317 N.C. 502, 510, 346 S.E.2d 441, 446 (1986).

24. G.S. 7B-310.

25. *See* Julie M. Arnold, Note, *"Divine" Justice and the Lack of Secular Intervention: Abrogating the Clergy–Communicant Privilege in Mandatory Reporting Statutes to Combat Child Sexual Abuse*, 42 VAL. U. L. REV. 849 (2008); J. Michael Keel, Comment, *Law and Religion Collide Again: The Priest–Penitent Privilege in Child Abuse Reporting Cases*, 28 CUMB. L. REV. 681 (1997).

26. *See* Rebecca R. S. Socolar, Desmond K. Runyan, and Lisa Amaya-Jackson, "Methodological and Ethical Issues Related to Studying Child Maltreatment," *Journal of Family Issues* 16, no. 5 (Sept. 1995): 565–86.

27. Section 301(d) of the Public Health Service Act (42 U.S.C. § 241(d)).

28. *See* DHHS, Office of Extramural Research, National Institutes of Health (NIH), *Certificates of Confidentiality Kiosk*, http://grants.nih.gov/grants/policy/coc/.

29. See the link under *Certificates of Confidential Information* entitled "Frequently Asked Questions: Certificates of Confidentiality," on the NIH web page cited in full in note 28, or go directly to http://grants.nih.gov/grants/policy/coc/faqs.htm.

Chapter 7

Deciding to Report

Cause to Suspect

What does it mean for a person to have "cause to suspect" that a child is abused, neglected, or dependent? Answering that question means looking at a combination of objective and personal factors. A mere feeling or suspicion that one cannot connect to something observable, to something the child or someone else has said, or to the child's behavior probably is not enough to trigger a duty to report. The standard is not just a suspicion but *cause to suspect*.[1] However, a person deciding whether to make a report also must consider a child's statements, appearance, or behavior (or other objective indicators) in light of the context; the person's experience; and other available information. A person who has cause to suspect that a child is abused, neglected, or dependent has no duty to conduct an investigation to uncover evidence for the report. He or she is not required to have actual knowledge of abuse, neglect, or dependency, and physical evidence is not required.

The North Carolina Supreme Court has acknowledged that determining cause to suspect child abuse or neglect involves some subjectivity. The court described the phrase "cause to suspect" as "giv[ing] wide margin to whatever prompts the reporter to notify DSS."[2] Contrasting the phrase with the wording in some other states' laws (for example, "reasonable cause to believe or suspect"), the court stated that the phrase "does not call for scrutiny, analysis, or judgment by a finder of fact."[3] Although determining that one has cause to suspect abuse or neglect involves both objective and subjective factors, someone who has cause to suspect has no discretion about whether to make a report. The North Carolina Court of Appeals made that point when it said that a law enforcement officer was not permitted "to weigh the safety interests of the public" or other discretionary factors before reporting possible sexual abuse.[4]

Some states' statutes define "cause to suspect" or similar phrases used in their reporting laws.[5] Montana, for example, defines "reasonable cause to suspect" as "cause that would lead a reasonable person to believe that child abuse or neglect may have occurred or is occurring, based on all the facts and circumstances known to the person."[6] Pennsylvania's statute refers to reasonable cause to suspect "on the basis of medical, professional or other training and experience."[7] In Alaska, "reasonable cause to suspect" means "cause, based on all the facts and circumstances known to the person, that would lead a reasonable person to believe that something might be the case."[8]

Appellate court decisions that address "cause to suspect" or similar phrases used in states' reporting laws usually involve allegations that someone either failed to report when a report was required[9] or made a report when there was no cause to suspect that abuse or neglect had occurred.[10] Few cases analyze the specific meaning of the phrase. A Michigan court, rejecting a claim that the state's reporting law was unconstitutionally vague, concluded that the words "'reasonable cause to suspect' speak for themselves and provide fair notice of the conduct expected in reporting suspected child abuse."[11] "[A] statute is not vague," the court said, "when the meaning of the words . . . can be fairly ascertained by reference to judicial determinations, the common law, dictionaries, treatises or even the words themselves, if they possess a common and generally accepted meaning."[12]

Two authors, on the other hand, have written about the inconsistencies in reporting that are caused by the lack of precision in statutory thresholds for requiring reports.[13] They assert the need to connect those thresholds to some system for making educated estimates of probability that abuse or neglect has occurred and the need for empirical research to support such a system.[14]

For most people, the imprecise threshold for the duty to report is not a major issue. Making a report in good faith, even if a report was not required, cannot be the basis for civil or criminal liability.[15] Although they are protected by the same immunity provisions, those who are bound by legal, professional, or ethical duties of confidentiality struggle to understand the line between required reports and prohibited disclosures. In some cases, that line can be determined only if a judicial, licensing, or other authority is called on to consider a claim based on failing to report or on making an improper disclosure.

Guidelines

In most situations, someone who has read the Juvenile Code definitions carefully will be able to tell whether there is cause to suspect that one or more of them apply to a particular child. Still, the definitions leave room for uncertainty. In the absence of formal clarification through legislation, court decisions, or state policy, local guidelines can help relieve this uncertainty and answer questions about the duty to report. Some counties have guidelines (sometimes called protocols) for cooperation between the county social services department and one or more other agencies or institutions. Ideally, local guidelines should be developed jointly by representatives of the county social services department and other key agencies in the community. Inquiries about local guidelines or protocols should be directed to individual county departments of social services.[16] (See Chapter 14 for an outline of suggested guidelines for cooperation between county departments of social services and local school units.)

With or without local guidelines, there will be circumstances in which individuals and institutions disagree about the definitions or struggle to determine whether they apply and whether a report is required. For example, a psychologist may wonder whether a report to social services is required if he learns that a client's girlfriend is punishing the client's child by locking him in a dark closet for up to forty-five minutes at a time. The girlfriend is in the home frequently but does not live there full time. Does that information give the psychologist cause to suspect that the child is an abused or neglected juvenile? The following questions must be considered:

- Is the girlfriend a "caretaker"? Is she "responsible for the health and welfare of [the child] in a residential setting," which is one of the criteria for being a caretaker?
- If the girlfriend is not a caretaker, is the child nevertheless abused or neglected because the child's father condoned or failed to prevent her mistreatment of the child?

- Does locking the child in a closet as discipline constitute abuse? Or neglect? Is the answer the same for a four-year-old child and a teenager? Is the answer the same if it happened once or if it happens regularly?

In cases of uncertainty about whether information or perceptions constitute cause to suspect that a child is abused, neglected, or dependent, the following basic guidelines may be helpful.

1. *Consider the purposes of the reporting law and of the child protective services system, which are to identify and respond to children who may need care, assistance, or protection when the child's parent (or guardian, custodian, or caretaker) either is not providing or cannot provide for those needs. Keep in mind that a primary part of the response is to assist parents to become better care providers for their children, and that children are removed from their homes only when it is not safe for them to remain at home.*

Ask yourself whether, in the situation being considered, involuntary intervention by the state (through the county social services department and possibly the court) is consistent with those purposes. Of course, if the definition of abuse, neglect, or dependency clearly applies, a report is required without further analysis.

2. *Do not limit your thinking to only one definition.*

If a child is harmed or placed at risk by someone who is not a parent, guardian, custodian, or caretaker, consider whether one of those persons has placed the child at risk or failed to protect the child from the other person's mistreatment. Cause to suspect abuse or neglect can arise from a parent's failure to protect as well as from a parent's harming a child or placing a child at risk. If the non-parent's conduct constitutes an assault or some other crime, a person who knows about it could make a report to law enforcement officials. That report would not relieve the person of the duty to make a report to social services, however, if the child is abused, neglected, or dependent because a parent, guardian, custodian, or caretaker allowed another person to harm the child.

3. Finally, if in doubt, make the report.

While the legal definitions of abuse, neglect, dependency, caretaker, and other key terms are important, a person who is concerned about a child but in a quandary as to whether the definitions or a particular definition applies should make a report. If the report is made in good faith, there is no liability risk in reporting. (See Chapter 9.) If the child or family needs assistance, even if it turns out that a report was not required and the department of social services is not authorized to conduct an assessment—that is, the report is screened out—the department may be able to suggest other resources to which the reporter can either direct his or her concern or refer the family that needs assistance.

Notes

1. North Carolina General Statutes (hereinafter G.S.) § 7B-301. The North Carolina General Statutes can be viewed online at www.ncga.state.nc.us/gascripts/Statutes/StatutesTOC.pl.

2. Dobson v. Harris, 352 N.C. 77, 84 n.4, 530 S.E.2d 829, 836 n.4 (2000), *citing* Danny R. Veilleux, Annotation, *Validity, Construction, and Application of State Statute Requiring Doctor or Other Person to Report Child Abuse*, 73 A.L.R. 4th 782, § 18 (2000). *See also* Benjamin H. Levi and Sharon G. Portwood, *Reasonable Suspicion of Child Abuse: Finding a Common Language*, 39 J.L. MED. & ETHICS 62 (2011) (hereinafter *Reasonable Suspicion*), http://onlinelibrary.wiley.com/doi/10.1111/j.1748-720X.2011.00550.x/pdf.

3. *Dobson*, 352 N.C. at 84 n.4, 530 S.E.2d at 836 n.4.

4. Smith v. Jackson Cnty. Bd. of Educ., 168 N.C. App. 452, 462, 608 S.E.2d 399, 408–09 (2005).

5. State statutes use a variety of wording to specify the standard for reporting—reason to believe, cause to believe, reasonable cause to believe, reasonable grounds to believe, reasonably believe, suspect, reason to suspect, cause to suspect, reasonable cause to suspect, reasonably suspect, and reasonable suspicion. Levi and Portwood, *Reasonable Suspicion*, cited in full in note 2, at 64.

6. MONT. CODE ANN. § 41-3-102(25).

7. 23 PA. CONS. STAT. § 6311(a).

8. ALASKA STAT. § 47.17.290(14).

9. *See, e.g.,* Gaines *ex rel.* Hancox v. Cumberland Cnty. Hosp. Sys., Inc., 203 N.C. App. 213, 224, 692 S.E.2d 119, 126 (2010) (reversing summary judgment in favor of a hospital and medical personnel in a negligence action and describing medical testimony that a child's injuries should have created cause to suspect child abuse and resulted in a report to social services); Diana G-D *ex rel.* Ann D. v. Bedford Cent. Sch. Dist., 33 Misc. 3d 970, 986–87, 932 N.Y.S.2d 316, 328–29 (2011) (holding that school

officials did not have cause to suspect child abuse and were not required to make a report when they were told third-hand by another child's mother about something the child allegedly said to other children on the playground, they observed no signs of abuse and no behavioral issues with the child, and the child seemed happy and denied that there were issues at home).

10. *See, e.g.,* Dobson v. Harris, 352 N.C. 77, 84, 530 S.E.2d 829, 836 (2000) (holding that a store employee's report to social services after the plaintiff reportedly yelled at her child, picked her up from the counter where she was sitting, and slammed her back down was entitled to the presumption of good faith and immunity for complying with the reporting law).

11. People v. Cavaiani, 172 Mich. App. 706, 714, 432 N.W.2d 409, 413 (1988) (holding that a psychologist was required to report a nine-year-old client's statement that her father had fondled her breasts, even though the psychologist, after talking with the father, personally believed that no abuse had occurred). *See also* Michigan Judicial Institute, *Child Protective Proceedings Benchbook: A Guide to Abuse and Neglect Cases,* 4th ed. (2013), § 2.2, http://courts.mi.gov/education/mji/Publications/Documents/Child-Protective-Proceedings.pdf.

12. *Cavaiani,* 172 Mich. App. at 714, 432 N.W.2d at 413 (citation omitted).

13. Levi and Portwood, *Reasonable Suspicion,* cited in full in note 2, at 62–69.

14. *Id.*

15. G.S. 7B-309.

16. Information about how to contact any of the one hundred county departments of social services in the state can be found at N. C. Department of Health and Human Services, *Local County Directory,* www.ncdhhs.gov/dss/local.

Chapter 8

How to Report

A report to the county department of social services may be made in person, by telephone, or in writing. It must be made to the department of social services in the county where the child resides or is found. Even if a child's legal residence is in another county, it is appropriate to make a report to the social services department in the county were the child is physically present. If the child's legal residence is in another county, the social services department that receives the report must notify the social services department in the county of the child's residence, and the directors of the two departments are required to "coordinate efforts to ensure that appropriate actions are taken."[1]

In North Carolina, each of the one hundred counties has a county department of social services or its equivalent.[2] All departments have the capacity to receive and respond to reports twenty-four hours a day, seven days a week. A person making a call outside regular office hours should ask for the on-call social worker. Some departments' after-hours numbers are dispatch numbers for local law enforcement agencies. In an emergency, or in any circumstance in which a person who needs to make a report does not know how to contact, or has trouble contacting, the social services department, the reporter should call 911 or a local law enforcement agency. All law enforcement agencies are aware of the duty to contact social services when they receive reports of child abuse, neglect, or dependency.

The information that must be reported will include the same information that creates the person's cause to suspect that a child is abused, neglected, or dependent. The report should include any information that would be helpful in determining whether the department of social services, the court, or both need to take action to protect or assist the child.

What to Include

The report should include as much of the following as the person making the report knows:

- the child's name, age, and address;
- the name and address of the child's parent, guardian, custodian, or caretaker;
- the names and ages of other children in the home;
- the child's location if the child is not at the home address;
- the nature and extent of any injury or condition resulting from abuse, neglect, or dependency; and
- any other information that might help establish the need for protective services or court intervention.[3]

Anonymous Reports

The law also requires the person who makes a report to give his or her name, address, and telephone number.[4] If the person does not provide that information, however, the department of social services still must conduct an assessment.[5] Occasionally people mistakenly interpret the department's duty to respond to anonymous reports as legal authority for making anonymous reports. A person's failure to identify himself or herself when making a report is a violation of the reporting law. In addition, it may prevent the department of social services from obtaining important information. An anonymous report also may generate questions about the motivation for the report or doubts as to its reliability.

Of course, a person who reports anonymously gives up the right to be notified about how the report is handled and the right to be informed of certain appeal procedures. (See Chapters 9 and 12 for more information on notification and review procedures.)

Reports by Institutions

The duty to report applies to institutions as well as individuals. Hospitals, schools, day care facilities, law enforcement agencies, and similar institutions should develop clear procedures to ensure that reporting occurs when it is required. Some institutions designate a liaison person through whom reports from staff can be channeled to the department of social services. That can be an acceptable way to comply with the law, but only if the following conditions are met:

1. The liaison must serve, in fact, as a channel for conveying reports and not as a screener of reports by others who believe they have cause to suspect abuse, neglect, or dependency.
2. The individual teacher, nurse, or other employee who is the source of the report must have assurance
   - that the liaison will convey the report to social services accurately and promptly, and
   - that the individual also is free to communicate personally with staff at the department of social services.

Reports about a Child in Another State

Each state's reporting law applies only within that state's boundaries. Sometimes, though, a person in North Carolina will know or suspect that a child who resides or is located in another state is an "abused," "neglected," or "dependent" juvenile, as those terms are defined in North Carolina law. The reporting law in North Carolina does not address these situations specifically, but it also does not include language restricting the duty to report to cases of children within the state. Common sense, state social services policy, and the purposes of the reporting law suggest the following guidance for making reports.

Regardless of the child's legal residence, if the child is present in North Carolina or the suspected abuse or neglect occurred in this state, a person in North Carolina who has cause to suspect that a child is abused, neglected, or dependent should make a report to a county department of social services in North Carolina. The report should be made to the department of social services in the county where the child is located if the child is here. If the child is no longer in the state, the report should be made to the department of social services in the county where the abuse or neglect may have occurred.

For example, if a child who resides in New York comes to North Carolina to visit a non-custodial parent, someone who suspects that the child is abused, neglected, or dependent should make a report to a county department of social services here, regardless of where the suspected abuse or neglect took place and regardless of whether the child has returned to his or her home state. Similarly, if a child is brought to North Carolina for medical treatment and hospital staff suspect that the child's injuries are the result of abuse, neglect, or dependency, a report should be made to the social services department in the county where the hospital is located.

Someone in North Carolina may have cause to suspect that a child in another state, who has never been in North Carolina, is abused, neglected, or dependent based on statements by the child's parents, photographs, or the child's own statements in a letter or telephone conversation. That person should make a report to the social services department in the county where he or she is located in North Carolina.

In each of these circumstances, both initial contact and appropriate follow-up with the child protective services agency in another state can be made more efficiently and effectively by a North Carolina county department of social services than by the individual who has cause to suspect the child's abuse, neglect, or dependency. The county social services department can facilitate appropriate communication between that individual and the agency in the other state when that is appropriate.[6]

Reports about Missing Children

Children of any age may disappear or go missing for a variety of reasons, only some of which involve the child's being abused, neglected, or dependent. Anyone who has cause to suspect that a child has disappeared and is abused, neglected, or dependent must of course make a report to the county department of social services. In addition, unrelated to the Juvenile Code and its reporting requirement, *any person who reasonably suspects* that a child under the age of sixteen has disappeared and may be in danger must make a report to law enforcement.[7] Failing to report the suspicion to law enforcement within a reasonable time is a Class 1 misdemeanor.[8]

For purposes of this reporting duty, a child has disappeared when a parent or other person supervising the child

1. does not know where the child is and
2. has not had contact with the child for twenty-four hours.[9]

Anyone who reports to law enforcement a suspicion that a child has disappeared has immunity from liability for making the report if the report was made in good faith.[10]

It is a Class I felony and the penalty for failing to report is greater when a parent or other person supervising a child knowingly or wantonly fails to report to law enforcement the disappearance of a child younger than sixteen.[11] In addition, that person's failure to report is considered a "grossly negligent omission" for purposes of the felony child abuse statute, and if the failure to report results in serious physical injury to the child, the person is guilty of a Class H felony.[12]

The duty to report a suspicion that a child has disappeared does not apply to a teacher with respect to a child's absences from school if the teacher reports the absences as required by applicable school law [Chapter 115C, Article 26, of the North Carolina General Statutes (hereinafter G.S.)].[13]

Also exempted from this reporting duty are operators and staff of a child care facility (or adults present in a facility with the provider's approval) when they already have a duty to report to law enforcement if a child under the age of sixteen who was placed in the facility's care is missing.[14] This reporting duty is set out in G.S. 110-102.1. A child care facility operator who willfully violates the duty, while caring for three or more children for more than four hours per day on two consecutive days, is guilty of a Class I felony.[15] Any person whose failure to report causes serious injury to the missing child is guilty of a Class H felony.[16]

Notes

1. North Carolina General Statutes (hereinafter G.S.) § 7B-302(a2). The North Carolina General Statutes can be viewed online at www.ncga.state.nc.us/gascripts/Statutes/StatutesTOC.pl. *See also* N.C. Department of Health & Human Services, Division of Social Services, "Reports Involving a Child Who Lives in Another County/State," *in* Section 1407.II.B.5, Chapter VIII, of the Division's online *Family Support and Child Welfare Manual* (hereinafter *State Manual*), http://info.dhhs.state.nc.us/olm/manuals/dss/csm-60/man/CS1407.pdf.

2. Social services and other human services programs are organized somewhat differently in Wake County, Mecklenburg County, and several other counties pursuant to authority given to boards of county commissioners under G.S. 153A-77. Information about each county social services department can be found at www.ncdhhs.gov/dss/local.

3. G.S. 7B-301.

4. *Id.*

5. *Id. See also* N.C. Admin. Code tit. 10A, subch. 70A, § .0105(a) (Apr. 2003) (stating that the social services director "shall receive and initiate an investigation on all reports of suspected child abuse, neglect, or dependency, including anonymous reports").

6. *See* "Reports Involving a Child Who Lives in Another County/State," *in* Section 1407.II, Chapter VIII, *State Manual*, cited in full in note 1, http://info.dhhs.state.nc.us/olm/manuals/dss/csm-60/man/CS1407-01.htm. Also see "Out-of-State Situations," *in* Section 1427.IV, Chapter VIII, *State Manual*, cited in full in note 1, discussing interstate situations in relation to the Responsible Individuals List (described in Chapter 11), http://info.dhhs.state.nc.us/olm/manuals/dss/csm-60/man/CS1427-03.htm#P127_9601.

7. G.S. 14-318.5(c). S.L. 2013-52 enacted G.S. 14-318.5 and made it effective December 1, 2013.

8. *Id.*

9. G.S. 14-318.5(a).

10. G.S. 14-318.5(g).

11. G.S. 14-318.5(b).

12. G.S. 14-318.4(a5), (a6).

13. G.S. 14-318.5(e).

14. G.S. 14-318.5(d).

15. G.S. 110-103(b)(2).

16. G.S. 110-103(c).

Chapter 9

Legal Rights of the Reporter

Confidentiality

The law directs county departments of social services to hold "in strictest confidence" the information they receive in reports and during assessments of child abuse, neglect, and dependency, including the identity of the reporter.[1] This confidentiality requirement is far from absolute, however. Social services departments are allowed to share information and a summary of documentation from a child protective services record with

- agencies or individuals providing or facilitating the provision of services to the child; and
- the prosecutor, when he or she needs the information in order to carry out mandated responsibilities resulting from the report.[2]

The child and the child's attorney may access the record, and the court in a juvenile case or in a separate civil or criminal action may order the social services director to disclose protective services records.[3] Even without a court order the social services department may voluntarily disclose to other parties in a juvenile abuse, neglect, or dependency case information that is relevant to the case, but it may not disclose

- the identity of the reporter;
- identifying information that would lead to the discovery of the reporter's identity; or
- the identity of any other person, if the department determines that disclosing the person's identity would endanger that person's life or safety.[4]

A reporter's identity might not be protected if he or she has information that has to be presented in court. The reporter could be called as a witness, although ordinarily the reporter would not have to reveal the fact that he or she was the person who made the report. The department of social services also may reveal the reporter's identity to a law enforcement agency that needs it in carrying out law enforcement's duties in relation to a report.[5] More generally, a social services department may disclose the reporter's identity to any federal, state, or local government entity that shows it needs to know the reporter's name in order to carry out its mandated responsibilities.[6]

In one situation the law specifically authorizes a judge to require a county social services director to reveal in court the identity of the person who made a report. If someone obstructs or interferes with a department's assessment after a report of suspected abuse, neglect, or dependency, the department may apply to the court for an order directing that person to stop obstructing or interfering with the assessment. At a hearing to determine whether the judge should issue that order, the judge may require the director of social services (or the director's representative) to identify the person who made the report.[7]

The circumstances that give the reporter cause to suspect abuse, neglect, or dependency may make it quite obvious to parents or others where a report originated. For that reason, some people choose to tell the parents (or guardian, custodian, or caretaker) that they are making a report, why they are making it, and something about what the parents can expect to happen as a result of the report. In some situations the person making the report can help the parent understand that the purpose of the report and any ensuing assessment by social services is to protect or assist the child. (There is no guarantee, however, that a criminal investigation will not occur.) Some parents may be less likely to confront, accuse, or harbor anger toward the reporter and may be more cooperative in an assessment if the reporter explains his or her actions and the reasons for them.

Obviously, the reporter should not tell the parent about the report if there is a possibility that doing so would lead to the parent's harming the child or someone else or would impede the social services department's assessment.

Immunity for Reporting, Cooperating, or Testifying

Many reports of suspected abuse, neglect, and dependency that social services departments receive prove to be either unfounded or impossible to substantiate. In state fiscal year 2010–2011, for example, departments of social services in North Carolina received 70,631 reports, involving 129,510 children.[8] Slightly fewer than half (34,767) of the reports resulted in findings of abuse, neglect, dependency, or a need for services.[9] A person who has cause to suspect that a child is abused, neglected, or dependent but has no proof may fear that he or she could be sued for making a report if a social services assessment finds no cause for concern. The law requires a person in that situation to make a report and does not require the person to produce evidence or proof of any kind. The law does not allow the person to delay reporting because he or she is not certain that the child is abused, neglected, or dependent.

The law encourages prompt reporting and acknowledges people's concerns about liability by providing immunity from legal liability for people who report in good faith. It also provides immunity to people who cooperate in a social services department's assessment (by sharing information, for example) or who testify in court actions that result from a report.[10]

> Anyone who makes a report pursuant to [the reporting law], cooperates with the county department of social services in a protective services assessment, testifies in any judicial proceeding resulting from a protective services report or assessment, or otherwise participates in the program authorized by [the law that provides for reports, assessments, and the provision of protective services], is immune from any civil or criminal liability that might otherwise be incurred or imposed for that action provided that the person was acting in good faith. In any proceeding involving liability, good faith is presumed.[11]

This provision was applied in a case in which a school principal reported to the department of social services his suspicion that a substitute teacher had abused students. The social services department reported the information to law enforcement officials, who conducted an investigation and charged the teacher with five counts of assault. After the teacher was found not guilty of all the charges in criminal court, he sued the city school system for malicious prosecution, defamation, intentional infliction of emotional distress, and negligence. Relying on the immunity provision and the statutory presumption of good faith, the trial court dismissed the teacher's case before it even went to trial. The court of appeals affirmed the trial court's decision.[12] To prevail in that situation a teacher would have to allege and prove that the report was made with actual malice.

In the case just described, the principal had reported not only to the department of social services, but also to the assistant superintendent for personnel. The trial court and the court of appeals applied the immunity provision and presumption of good faith to that report as well. The appellate court said:

> [A] report made in good faith by the principal of the school to his or her superior who is responsible for school personnel would clearly fall within the scope of the immunity contemplated by the statute. To say that the principal was protected in reporting the incident to the Department of Social Services but not in reporting to the Assistant Superintendent would be both contrary to the spirit of the statute and also impractical.[13]

The law cannot prevent an irate parent or others from suing people who report suspected child abuse or neglect or who testify in court or cooperate in protective services assessments. The Juvenile Code's immunity provisions, however, make it much less likely that suits will be filed or that a suit, once filed, will succeed. In order to establish liability, the person who sues would have to prove, among other things, that whoever made the report, testified, or cooperated in an assessment did so "in bad faith"— that is, without any justification other than malice.[14]

The North Carolina Supreme Court has stated that the legislative intent of the immunity provision is to encourage people to "be vigilant in assuring the safety and welfare of the [state's] children"—a policy that "compels a significant evidentiary burden for those who challenge the presumption that people who report . . . abuse or neglect do so in good faith."[15]

Notification and Review

The law and state administrative rules require a county department of social services to give a person who reports suspected abuse, neglect, or dependency certain information about the department's response to the report.[16]

Within five days after receiving a report, the department must give the person who made the report written notice of

1. whether the department accepts the report and is conducting an assessment or plans to initiate an assessment[17] and
2. whether the department has referred the report to a state or local law enforcement agency.

Every person who makes a report is entitled to this notice unless he or she reports anonymously or specifically requests not to receive it.

If the department does not accept a report for assessment, the notice described above also must inform the person who made the report of

- the basis for the decision not to accept the report,
- the person's right to request a departmental review of the decision,
- the procedures for requesting a review of the decision,
- the identity of the persons who would review the decision, and
- the manner in which a review would be conducted.[18]

If the department does accept the report for assessment, the department must give the person who made the report a second written notice within five days after completing the assessment. This notice must tell the reporter

- whether the department found abuse, neglect, or dependency;
- what (if any) action the department is taking to protect the child;
- whether the department has filed a petition to begin a juvenile court action; and
- how to request a review by the local prosecutor of a decision by the department not to file a petition.[19]

This notice is required for every report the department accepts for assessment, unless the person who made the report did so anonymously or specifically requested not to receive it.[20]

The screening of reports is discussed in Chapter 11. Rights of review are described in more detail in Chapter 12.

Notes

1. North Carolina General Statutes (hereinafter G.S.) § 7B-302(a1). The North Carolina General Statutes can be viewed online at www.ncga.state.nc.us/gascripts/Statutes/StatutesTOC.pl. The law does not specify any remedy for a reporter whose identity is disclosed improperly or any penalty for making an improper disclosure.

2. N.C. Admin. Code (hereinafter N.C.A.C.) tit. 10A, subch. 70A, § .0113 (Sept. 1991).

3. *See* G.S. 7B-302(a1); N.C.A.C. tit. 10A, subch. 70A, § .0113(a) (Sept. 1991).

4. G.S. 7B-700(a).

5. N.C.A.C. tit. 10A, subch. 70A, § .0105(c) (Apr. 2003). This rule specifically authorizes social services to share with law enforcement the name, address, and telephone number of the person making the report when that information is necessary in order for law enforcement to perform its duties related to the report.

6. G.S. 7B-302(a1)(1a).

7. G.S. 7B-303(e). These are not the exclusive means by which a reporter's identity might be revealed. For example, the Health Insurance Portability and Accountability Act of 1996, 42 U.S.C. §§ 1320d–1320d-9 (2010) (HIPAA), allows patients and their representatives to obtain an "accounting of disclosures." (*See* 45 C.F.R. § 164.528.) Because a parent ordinarily is a minor patient's representative, this means that a health care provider who reports suspected abuse, neglect, or dependency must maintain a record of the report and provide it to the parent upon request. However, the provider may choose not to treat the parent as the child's representative if the provider reasonably believes that the parent has abused or neglected the child or that treating the parent as the child's personal representative could endanger the child. (*See* 45 C.F.R. § 164.502(g)(5).)

8. These and other child welfare statistics for North Carolina are from D. F. Duncan, H. C. Kum, K. A. Flair, C. J. Stewart, J. Vaughn, R. Bauer, and A. You, *Management Assistance for Child Welfare, Work First, and Food & Nutrition Services in North Carolina* (hereinafter *Management Assistance*) (Chapel Hill, N.C.: UNC Jordan Institute for Families), http://ssw.unc.edu/ma/.

9. *Management Assistance*, cited in full in note 8.

10. G.S. 7B-309.

11. *Id.*

12. Davis v. Durham City Schs., 91 N.C. App. 520, 372 S.E.2d 318 (1988).

13. *Id.* at 523, 372 S.E.2d at 320. The parties did not raise, and the court did not discuss, the issues of whether a substitute teacher was a caretaker and whether a report to social services had even been required. When this case arose, the Juvenile Code definition of "caretaker" did not specify, as it does now [*see* G.S. 7B-101(3)], that it refers only to individuals providing care "in a residential setting," and there was some uncertainty as to whether incidents involving school personnel should be reported to social services.

14. For a case in which the court found that a report to social services was made with malice, see *Kroh v. Kroh*, 152 N.C. App. 347, 567 S.E.2d 760 (2002), *review denied*, 356 N.C. 673, 577 S.E.2d 120 (2003), which held that a wife's statements to a social

services department that her husband had molested their two children were made with actual malice.

15. Dobson v. Harris, 352 N.C. 77, 78, 530 S.E.2d 829, 832 (2000) (holding that the trial court properly dismissed a parent's action against a department store and a store employee who made a report to social services after observing the parent yell at the child, pick the child up from a counter, and slam her back down).

16. G.S. 7B-302; N.C.A.C. tit. 10A, subch. 70A, §§ .0105(h) (Apr. 2003) and .0109 (Sept. 1994).

17. G.S. 7B-302(f). Note that every social services department must have a procedure for a two-level internal review that includes, at a minimum, the social worker and the worker's supervisor before making a decision not to accept a report. N.C.A.C. tit. 10A, subch. 70A, § .0105(g) (Apr. 2003).

18. N.C.A.C. tit. 10A, subch. 70A, § .0105(h) (Apr. 2003).

19. G.S. 7B-302(g).

20. *Id.*

Chapter 10

Consequences of Failing to Report

Criminal Liability

For many years North Carolina differed from most other states by having no statute imposing civil or criminal penalties for failing to comply with its mandatory reporting law.[1] As of August 2012, North Carolina was one of only three states without statutory sanctions for willfully failing to make a report when the law required one.[2] Although the General Assembly enacted the state's first mandatory reporting law in 1971 and has amended it several times, the legislature did not establish a statutory penalty for failing to report until 2013.[3]

Effective December 1, 2013, it is a Class 1 misdemeanor for any person or institution to *knowingly* or *wantonly*

1. fail to make a report when the reporting law requires one, or
2. prevent another person from making a report when the law requires one.

In addition, it is a Class 1 misdemeanor for a county social services director who receives a report of sexual abuse of a child in a child care facility to *knowingly* fail to notify the State Bureau of Investigation.[4]

A person acts "knowingly" when the person knows what he or she is about to do and, with that knowledge, proceeds to act.[5] A person acts "wantonly" when he or she acts with conscious and intentional disregard of and indifference to the rights and safety of others.[6] Courts have said that "wantonly" has essentially the same meaning as "willfully," which means "the wrongful doing of an act without legal excuse or justification, or the commission of an act purposely and deliberately in violation of law."[7]

Even before enactment of a statute creating a criminal penalty for failing to report, there was some risk of criminal liability for violating North Carolina's reporting law. In the 1980s, at least two people in the state were prosecuted for violating the reporting law.[8] These cases were not appealed beyond the trial court level, so there were no appellate court decisions that served as precedent for other cases. The prosecutions were based on a seldom-used common law rule that if a statute does not specify consequences for failing to perform a duty created by the statute, a person who fails to perform that duty can be charged with a general misdemeanor.[9] Because North Carolina now has a statutory penalty for failing to report, this common law theory is no longer relevant.

Civil Liability

The threat of civil liability has materialized rarely in this state. Although civil actions have been filed alleging violations of the reporting law, no appellate court decisions in North Carolina deal directly with civil liability for failing to report suspected child abuse, neglect, or dependency.[10] That does not mean that a person cannot be civilly liable for failing to report child abuse in North Carolina. The issue simply is not addressed in statutes and has not been addressed directly by appellate courts in this state.

A number of courts in other states have considered the issue of liability for failing to report, with varying results. Those cases involve statutory schemes that differ from state to state, and their conclusions vary. For example, most courts have rejected the notion that the state's mandatory reporting law itself implies a right to bring a civil action against someone who violates the law.[11] A few, though, have held otherwise. The Supreme Court of Washington, interpreting a statute that mandates reporting by specified professionals, held that the state's reporting law "implies a cause of action against a mandatory reporter who fails to report suspected child abuse."[12]

The notion that violation of a statutory duty may form the basis for civil liability is a familiar one in North Carolina. Our courts have said that "when a statute imposes a duty on a person for the protection of others, it is a public safety statute and a violation of such a statute is negligence *per se*."[13] However, not every statutory duty that can be associated with safety automatically creates a claim for negligence when the duty is breached.[14] The courts have not spoken to the applicability of that principle to violations of the reporting law.[15]

Even if the reporting law itself does not create a civil cause of action for failing to report, application of the general principles of the law of negligence could result in liability.[16] Establishing a claim based on common law negligence requires the plaintiff to prove

- that the defendant had a duty of care to the plaintiff,
- that the defendant breached that duty,
- that the defendant's breach of duty was the actual or proximate cause of the injury to the plaintiff, and
- that the type of injury or harm suffered by the plaintiff was a foreseeable consequence of the defendant's breach of duty.[17]

Generally, the duty that every person owes to every other person is a duty of reasonable care under the circumstances to see that harm does not come to the other person. The existence of a statute creating a specific duty designed to protect a category of people may affect a court's assessment of what "reasonable care" is in a particular circumstance.[18] However, the court also would consider the statute's overall purposes in deciding whether the statute established the standard for reasonable care for purposes of negligence liability.[19]

Statutes that impose duties on law enforcement officers sometimes are treated differently. Courts have applied a doctrine known as the "public duty doctrine" to shield law enforcement officers from some liability claims based on alleged negligence, reasoning that the officers' duties are directed toward the protection of the public generally, not the protection of particular individuals. The court of appeals has held, however, that this doctrine does not protect an officer from a claim of negligence based on failing to report known child abuse, because the duty to report is not particular to law enforcement—it is a duty imposed by statute on everyone.[20]

If a court found that the reporting law set the minimum standard for reasonable care, liability for violating the reporting law still would exist only if the court also determined that a defendant's failure to report was the proximate cause of injury or harm to the child—that is, if the report had been made, the child most likely would not have been harmed. A case decided by the court of appeals in 2010 involved a child's claim that a hospital and other defendants who treated him for a wrist injury were negligent for failing to identify and report prior abuse the child had suffered.[21] After the child received treatment and returned home, he suffered a serious brain injury allegedly inflicted by his mother's boyfriend. The suit alleged that these injuries were caused by the defendants' negligence because had they followed proper screening procedures and identified the earlier abuse, a report would have been made to the department of social services and the department would have removed the child from the home. The trial court dismissed the case, and the court of appeals reversed, holding that the plaintiff's extensive medical evidence about the standard of care and causation was sufficient to withstand the defendants' motion to dismiss. In other words, the court held that a jury should determine "whether defendants' actions constituted a breach of the standard of care and proximately caused [the child's] injury."[22]

Other Consequences of Failing to Report

The most obvious and serious consequence of not reporting suspected child abuse, neglect, or dependency is that a child may suffer unnecessarily. The cost to the child, the family, and ultimately to society may be immense— especially when compared with the small effort required to make a report that may result in protection for the child. In some cases, of course, the consequences of not reporting may be insignificant. The suspicion may be unfounded, the department of social services may be involved already, or someone else may have made a report. But there is no way of predicting whether the report will make a difference in a child's life, and the law does not excuse a person from the duty to report for any of these or similar reasons.

In some instances a failure to report may place a person's professional credentials or employment in jeopardy. In reviewing the revocation of a psychologist's license based on multiple alleged violations of the Ethical Principles of Psychologists, the court of appeals held that the psychologist "technically" had violated both one of the ethical principles and the child abuse reporting law by failing to report suspected child abuse.[23] In response to the psychologist's argument that he had not reported because "he thought the matter was already in the judicial system and the parents and attorneys knew of the alleged sexual abuse," the court of appeals stated that the reporting law "makes no exceptions for extenuating circumstances in reporting suspected child abuse."[24]

North Carolina law relating to civil and criminal liability for failing to report suspected child abuse, neglect, or dependency remains relatively undeveloped. To encourage people to report, the Juvenile Code has relied primarily on the policies underlying the reporting requirement, the ease of reporting, and the provision of immunity for good-faith reporting—rather than on fear of civil liability or criminal prosecution for failing to report. Now, the possibility of criminal prosecution for knowingly or wantonly failing to report adds a substantial additional incentive to comply with the reporting law.

Notes

1. The committee that drafted the Juvenile Code that was in effect from 1980 to 1999 said in its 1979 report:

> The Committee considered a penalty for not reporting abuse, neglect, or dependency to insure that the administrators of hospitals, schools, and other institutions whose employees may see evidence of abuse, neglect, or dependence develop a mechanism for reporting and encourage their employees to report such incidents as required by law. The Committee, however, concluded that the threat of civil suit for failure to report should be sufficient incentive for institutions to encourage reporting.

Juvenile Code Revision Committee, *The Final Report of the Juvenile Code Revision Committee* (Raleigh, N.C.: North Carolina Department of Crime Control and Public Safety, Jan. 1979), 34–35.

2. U.S. Department of Health & Human Services, Administration for Children & Families, Child Welfare Information Gateway, "Penalties for Failure to Report and False Reporting of Child Abuse and Neglect," August 2012, www.childwelfare.gov/ systemwide/laws_policies/statutes/report.cfmall.pdf. *See also* Seth C. Kalichman, *Mandated Reporting of Suspected Child Abuse: Ethics, Law, & Policy*, 2nd ed. (hereinafter *Mandated Reporting of Suspected Child Abuse*) (Washington, D.C.: American Psychological Association, 1999), 33–42.

3. *See* S.L. 2013-52, sec. 7.

4. S.L. 2013-52, sec. 7, rewrote the reporting law, G.S. 7B-301, to create these offenses.

5. *See, e.g.*, State v. Williams, ___ N.C. App. ___, 741 S.E.2d 9, 19 (2013).

6. Jessica Smith, *North Carolina Crimes: A Guidebook on the Elements of Crime*, 7th ed. (Chapel Hill, N.C.: UNC School of Government, 2012), 6, *citing* State v. Brackett, 306 N.C. 138 (1982); State v. Williams, 284 N.C. 67 (1973).

7. *Id.* at 6–7, *citing* State v. Arnold, 264 N.C. 348 (1965).

8. *See* State v. Freitag, Wake Cnty. Dist. Ct., Jan. 31, 1986; State v. Gray, Durham Cnty. Dist. Ct., Feb. 1986, and Durham Cnty. Super. Ct., Jan. 14, 1987. *See also* "Assistant

Superintendent Convicted for Not Reporting Suspected Child Abuse," *School Law Bulletin* 17 (Spring 1986): 46–47, and "Charges against Chapel Hill Psychologist Dismissed," *Durham Morning Herald*, January 15, 1987, 1A. The *Gray* case is discussed at pages 36–37 *in* Kalichman, *Mandated Reporting of Suspected Child Abuse*, cited in full in note 1.

9. *See, e.g.*, State v. Bishop, 228 N.C. 371, 45 S.E.2d 858 (1947); State v. Bloodworth, 94 N.C. 918 (1886); State v. Parker, 91 N.C. 650 (1884).

10. The state court of appeals affirmed the trial court's dismissal of an action in which negligent failure to report child abuse was one of six claims against a school principal, but the appellate court's opinion made no mention of the specific claim relating to failure to report. Medlin v. Bass, 96 N.C. App. 410, 386 S.E.2d 80 (1989), *aff'd*, 327 N.C. 587, 398 S.E.2d 460 (1990). In a case brought by former minor patients of a state hospital, the court of appeals affirmed the trial court's grant of summary judgment in favor of the defendants, finding among other things that one incident of offensive touching of a minor patient by a male staff member did not constitute abuse that had to be reported. Susan B. v. Planavsky, 60 N.C. App. 77, 298 S.E.2d 397 (1982), *review denied*, 307 N.C. 702, 301 S.E.2d 388 (1983). A civil action in which one claim asserted was that school officials were negligent in failing to report child abuse was filed in Onslow County in 1986 by a student after he reached age eighteen, but the case was settled before it went to trial. Complaint on behalf of minor plaintiff, Hague v. Lloyd, No. 86-CVS-1347, Onslow Cnty. Super. Ct., filed Aug. 1, 1986.

11. *See, e.g.*, Doe *ex rel.* Doe v. Wal-Mart Stores, Inc., 393 S.C. 240, 711 S.E.2d 908 (2011) (holding that South Carolina's reporting law did not create a private right of action for negligence *per se*); Becker v. Mayo Found., 737 N.W.2d 200 (Minn. 2007) (holding that the reporting law did not create civil liability for failing to report); Arbaugh v. Bd. of Educ., Cnty. of Pendleton, 214 W. Va. 677, 682–83, 591 S.E.2d 235, 241 (2003) (concluding that West Virginia's reporting law did not create an implied private civil cause of action and citing cases from other states reaching the same conclusion).

12. Beggs v. Wash. Dep't of Soc. & Health Servs., 171 Wash. 2d 69, 77, 247 P.3d 421, 425 (2011). *See also* Ham v. Hosp. of Morristown, Inc., 917 F. Supp. 531 (E.D. Tenn. 1995) (holding that Tennessee's reporting statute created a private cause of action for failure of physicians and hospital personnel to recognize and report symptoms of child abuse).

13. Gregory v. Kilbride, 150 N.C. App. 601, 610, 565 S.E.2d 685, 692 (2002), *review denied*, 357 N.C. 164, 580 S.E.2d 365 (2003), *citing* McEwen Funeral Serv., Inc. v. Charlotte City Coach Lines, Inc., 248 N.C. 146, 102 S.E.2d 816 (1958) (additional citation omitted).

14. *Gregory*, 150 N.C. App. at 610, 565 S.E.2d at 692.

15. The court of appeals did hold in one case that violation of the statute prescribing a social services department's duties after receiving a report of suspected abuse or neglect could give rise to an action for negligence. Coleman v. Cooper, 89 N.C. App. 188, 197, 366 S.E.2d 2, 8 (1988), *aff'd in part, rev'd in part, remanded, as to individual defendant's liability*, 102 N.C. App. 650, 403 S.E.2d 577, *review denied*, 329 N.C. 786, 408 S.E.2d 517 (1991).

16. As early as 1976, a California court held that a doctor and hospital could be liable if their negligent failure to diagnose and report battered-child syndrome resulted in the child's being returned home and receiving further injuries. Landeros v. Flood, 17 Cal. 3d 399, 131 Cal. Rptr. 69, 551 P.2d 389 (1976).

17. *See, e.g.*, Davis v. N.C. Dep't of Human Res., 121 N.C. App. 105, 112, 465 S.E.2d 2, 6 (1995) (citations omitted), *review denied*, 343 N.C. 750, 473 S.E.2d 612 (1996).

18. *See, e.g., Gregory*, 150 N.C. App. at 610, 565 S.E.2d at 692 (noting that "[a] court may determine that a statute creates a minimum standard of care required to avoid liability for negligence").

19. *Id.* at 610, 565 S.E.2d at 692.

20. Smith v. Jackson Cnty. Bd. of Educ., 168 N.C. App. 452, 462, 608 S.E.2d 399, 407–08 (2005). The appellate court affirmed the trial court's denial of the officers' motion to dismiss and did not address the ultimate outcome of the negligence claim. For a discussion of the "special duty" and "special relationship" exceptions to the public duty doctrine, see *Blaylock v. North Carolina Department of Correction*, 200 N.C. App. 541, 685 S.E.2d 140 (2009), *review denied, dismissed*, 363 N.C. 853, 693 S.E.2d 916, 917 (2010). Also see North Carolina General Statutes § 143-299.1A, which sets out the limits on use of the public duty doctrine as an affirmative defense. The North Carolina General Statutes can be viewed online at www.ncga.state.nc.us/gascripts/Statutes/StatutesTOC.pl.

21. Gaines v. Cumberland Cnty. Hosp. Sys., 203 N.C. App. 213, 692 S.E.2d 119, *review denied*, 700 S.E.2d 750 (2010).

22. *Id.* at 227, 692 S.E.2d at 127.

23. White v. N.C. State Bd. of Exam'rs of Practicing Psychologists, 97 N.C. App. 144, 388 S.E.2d 148 (1990).

24. *Id.* at 165, 388 S.E.2d at 161.

Part 4. Assessment and Response

Chapter 11

Social Services Procedures

A report of abuse, neglect, or dependency results in certain actions by the county department of social services. In some cases local law enforcement agencies are involved as well. The juvenile (district) court may take action, but only when the department of social services files a petition after determining that a child needs to be removed from the home or that court intervention is needed for some other reason. Before any court action is initiated, the county social services department receives and screens reports, conducts assessments, and, in some cases, provides protective services.

Screening

When a county department of social services receives a report, it must answer the following question: If the information in the report is true, does the child fit into the Juvenile Code definition of "abused juvenile," "neglected juvenile," or "dependent juvenile"?[1] A report concerning any situation or person not covered by one of these definitions will be screened out, and the department will not conduct an assessment. If someone reported that her neighbors were beating their eighteen-year-old daughter, for example, the report would be screened out because the definition of juvenile does not include someone who is eighteen or older.[2] If an emergency room nurse reported to social services that a fourteen-year-old boy had been stabbed by another student at school, the department would screen the report out because the harm to the child was not caused or allowed by the child's parent, guardian, custodian, or caretaker.[3] Similarly, reports about children who are abused by religious officials, coaches, or teachers are screened out unless the responsible individual is the child's parent, guardian, custodian, or caretaker. A social services department that received such a report would not conduct an assessment. However, if the report indicated that the child had been "physically harmed in violation of any criminal statute" by someone other than the child's parent, guardian, custodian, or caretaker, the social services department would be required to relay the report to law enforcement authorities and to the district attorney.[4]

Often screening decisions are less clear-cut than the examples given above. When the decisions involve interpretations of the Juvenile Code definitions, counties may respond differently to very similar reports. Professionals or institutions, such as hospitals, that regularly make reports to more than one county must deal with different personnel and sometimes different procedures from county to county. In North Carolina each county department of social services operates its own child protective services program. Nevertheless, each county is governed by the same law and by the same detailed policies and procedures for each stage of a protective services case. The state Social Services Commission issues rules relating to child protective services.[5] The state Division of Social Services in the Department of Health and Human Services (DHHS) provides training for social workers and issues policy manuals and other guidance for county departments.[6]

A lengthy section of the Division of Social Services' child protective services manual establishes a structured intake process that emphasizes the extreme importance of intake, the need for consistency in intake decisions, and the importance of focusing early on families' strengths as well as on the problem that is reported.[7] While these policies provide fairly specific guidance, they do not answer all of the hard questions. Rather, they include interview and screening tools and suggestions about how to approach the difficult questions in ways that are consistent with the goal of child protection. Any social services department's decision to screen out a report of suspected abuse, neglect, or dependency must involve, at a minimum, both the social worker and his or her supervisor.[8] If a report is screened out, the department may try to refer the reporter to another appropriate agency or resource.

As discussed in Chapter 5, cases in which the definitions may be interpreted and applied differently often involve reports that come from schools, hospitals, and other professional settings. Situations that are susceptible to different interpretations underscore both the necessity of interagency coordination at the local level and the value of guidelines developed jointly by social services departments and the agencies and institutions that make reports frequently. Communities, not just social services departments, need to develop appropriate responses to drug-exposed infants, children with basic hygiene and clothing needs, children with school-attendance problems, and teenagers living apart from their families. Responses that make the best use of resources and provide the best protection for children may differ from county to county.

Notification after a Report Is Made
Notifying the Reporter
Within five working days after receiving a report, the department of social services must give the person who made the report written notice of

1. whether the report has been accepted for assessment, and
2. whether the report has been referred to the appropriate state or local law enforcement agency.[9]

This notice is required after every report of suspected abuse, neglect, or dependency unless the person who made the report either asks specifically that the department not provide the notice or fails to provide contact information that is sufficient for the department to provide the notice.

In addition, in any case in which the department does not accept a report for assessment, the notice must inform the reporter of

1. the fact that the department will not conduct an assessment,
2. the basis for that decision, and
3. the reporter's right to ask for a review of the decision and the procedures for making that request.[10]

(The review process is discussed in Chapter 12.)

A person whose report is accepted for assessment is entitled to a second notification when the assessment is completed. See "Notification Requirements at Conclusion of Assessment," below.

Notifying Law Enforcement

In some cases, after screening out a report, the social services director must make an immediate oral report, followed by a written report within forty-eight hours, to both the district attorney and an appropriate local law enforcement agency. These reports are required any time the information in the report indicates that a child may have been physically harmed in violation of any criminal law by someone other than the child's parent, guardian, custodian, or caretaker.[11] The social services department, for example, would not conduct an assessment based on a report that a substitute teacher had molested a child. The department would be required, however, to notify the district attorney and law enforcement authorities immediately after receiving the report.

The law enforcement agency then would be required to begin a criminal investigation immediately (and in no event more than forty-eight hours after being notified). After the investigation, the district attorney would decide whether any criminal charges should be filed.[12] See "Law Enforcement's Role," below, for discussion of other kinds of notification to law enforcement officials.

Notification When Report Involves Child Care

If a report relates to possible abuse or neglect of a child in a child care facility, the social services director must notify the state Department of Health and Human Services within twenty-four hours after receiving the report.[13] If the report involves possible sexual abuse of a child in a child care setting, the director also must notify the State Bureau of Investigation within this same time frame.[14]

A county social services director who receives a report of sexual abuse of a child in a child care facility and knowingly fails to notify the State Bureau of Investigation is guilty of a Class 1 misdemeanor.[15]

Social Services Assessment

Purpose of Assessment

The purposes of the social services department's assessment after a report of abuse, neglect, or dependency are to determine

- whether the child's needs for care and protection are being met and whether there is an immediate risk to the child's safety;
- the extent of any abuse or neglect;
- the risk of harm to the child;
- whether removal from the home is necessary for the child's protection;
- whether the child and family need protective services and, if they do, what services would be most helpful; and
- whether a petition should be filed to take the matter to juvenile court.[16]

The Multiple Response System adopted by the state divides assessment responses into two categories— a "family assessment response" and a traditional "investigative assessment response"[17] An investigative assessment occurs in response to a report of abuse or serious neglect. These cases present serious safety issues, possible criminal charges, or both. A family assessment response follows a report of neglect (other than serious neglect) or dependency. It focuses on identifying a family's strengths and needs and on engaging the family in efforts to become able to provide better care for the children. In these cases there may never be a substantiation that labels a child as having been abused or neglected. The emphasis instead is on whether the family needs services. Social services departments try to involve families and their relatives and communities directly in evaluating a family's needs and available resources and in planning for a child's safety and welfare.

Starting the Assessment

A social services department must refer a report to another county social services department for assessment if the report involves abuse, neglect, or dependency allegedly caused by an employee of the department, a foster parent supervised by the department, a member of the county social services board, or a caretaker in a sole-source contract group home or a child care facility operated by the department.[18] In addition, a social services director may ask another county to conduct an assessment any time that, in the director's professional judgment, the department would be perceived as having a conflict of interest in conducting the assessment.[19]

The county social services director, acting primarily through the local social services staff, is required to make a prompt and thorough assessment of every abuse, neglect, and dependency report that the department does not screen out or refer to another county. If the report alleges abuse, the assessment must start immediately (and in no event more than twenty-four hours after the department receives the report).[20] An assessment of a report of neglect or dependency must begin within seventy-two hours unless the report alleges abandonment, in which case the assessment must begin immediately.[21] Every assessment must include a visit to the place where the child lives unless the report involves abuse or neglect of a child in a child care facility.[22] However, when conducting an assessment, a social worker may enter a private residence only if

1. the social worker has a reasonable belief that a child in the home is in imminent danger of death or serious physical injury; or
2. the parent or other person responsible for the child's care consents to the entry;
3. the social worker is accompanied by a law enforcement officer who has legal authority to enter the residence; or
4. a court order authorizes entry.[23]

At the request of a county social services director, state or local law enforcement officers must assist with an assessment and with an evaluation of the seriousness of a report of abuse, neglect, or dependency.[24] However, the mere presence of a law enforcement officer is not sufficient to ensure entry into a private residence for purposes of an assessment. Without consent to enter, a law enforcement officer may enter only with a warrant or court order unless the officer reasonably believes that entering the residence is "urgently necessary to save life, prevent serious bodily harm, or avert or control public catastrophe."[25]

Steps in an Assessment

The first step in an assessment is to make face-to-face contact with the child, when that is possible.[26] An assessment also includes

- checking county and state records to determine whether other reports have been made concerning the same child or other children in the family;
- interviewing family members and others who might have relevant information;

- seeing any other children who live in the home; and
- when possible, interviewing any person who is reported to have abused or neglected the child.[27]

County social services departments use structured decision-making tools to determine how to characterize the outcome of an assessment and what (if any) actions are appropriate.[28] These tools include assessments that the department conducts with the family to evaluate safety and risks, identify the family's strengths and needs, and formulate an initial case plan.

The law requires the department of social services to make a prompt and thorough assessment, but it does not specify any length of time within which the department must complete the assessment. State social services policy states that a family assessment should be completed within forty-five days and an investigative assessment within thirty days, or the record should document a rationale for the assessment's extending beyond that time.[29]

At the conclusion of an investigatory assessment, which occurs when a report involves abuse or serious neglect, the department classifies the report as either *substantiated* or *unsubstantiated.* These terms are not defined in state law, policy, or regulations. Presumably a report is substantiated if the social services assessment reveals facts or evidence sufficient to establish that a child is "abused," "neglected," or "dependent" as the Juvenile Code defines those terms.[30] It is not clear, however, what standard the department should apply in determining whether the evidence and facts are sufficient.[31]

The department of social services conducts a family assessment when the report involves neglect or dependency but not abuse or serious neglect. The determination at the end of the assessment is one of the following:

- services needed;
- services provided, protective services no longer needed;
- services recommended; or
- services not recommended[32]

Confidential Information

In conducting an assessment, the director of the county department of social services (or the director's representative) may ask the person who made the report for additional information or records. The law authorizes the director to obtain, from the reporter or anyone else, information that the director considers relevant to a case, even if the information otherwise would be confidential.[33] Anyone who receives a social services director's written demand for records or information must provide the director with the information and with access to and copies of any records. Three kinds of information are excluded from this rule:

1. information that is protected by the attorney–client privilege,
2. any information that federal laws or regulations prohibit the person from disclosing,[34] and
3. criminal investigative records.[35]

The third exception applies, however, only if disclosure would jeopardize the assessment or trial of a criminal matter and the custodian of the records applies to the court and receives an order preventing disclosure.[36]

Assessment Following a Child's Death

When the department of social services receives a report that a child has died as a result of suspected maltreatment, it is required to

1. determine immediately whether other children are in the home and, if so,
2. conduct an immediate assessment to determine whether those children need services or need to be removed from the home for their protection.[37]

The department takes action as if a report of possible abuse, neglect, or dependency has been made regarding any other children in the same home. A criminal investigation, of course, is the responsibility of law enforcement.

Assessment in an Institutional Setting

When a social services department receives a report that a child in an institutional setting, such as a residential school or treatment facility, is an abused, neglected, or dependent juvenile or has died as the result of maltreatment, the department must conduct an assessment as in other cases. The department must immediately determine whether other children in the facility are subject to the care and supervision of someone allegedly responsible for the abuse, neglect, or death of the child who was the subject of the report. If so, the assessment must determine whether those children need protective services or should be removed from the facility for their protection.[38]

Law Enforcement's Role

In any case, the department of social services may consult with and seek assistance from a law enforcement agency. If asked to do so by the social services director, the law enforcement agency must assist in the assessment and in an evaluation of the seriousness of any report of abuse, neglect, or dependency.[39]

Whenever an assessment by a social services department reveals that a child may have been abused, the director of social services must make an oral report immediately and a written report within forty-eight hours to both the district attorney and the appropriate local law enforcement agency.[40] The law enforcement agency must begin a criminal investigation immediately (and in no event more than forty-eight hours after being notified) and must coordinate its investigation with the protective services assessment being done by social services.[41] When the criminal investigation is complete, the district attorney decides whether any criminal charges should be filed.

Social Services Action

Immediate Removal of Child

If the department's assessment results in a determination that a child is abused, neglected, or dependent, the director must assess whether the child will be safe if left in the home. Sometimes the parent will agree to a protection plan specifying actions the parent will take to ensure the child's safety. Sometimes a safety plan will include the parent's voluntary placement of the child with a relative or other person. If a parent does not consent, however, the department ordinarily must file a petition and obtain a court order before removing a child from the custody of a parent.

If it appears that the time it would take to file a petition and obtain a court order might result either in injury to the child or in the department's inability to take the child into custody later, then a law enforcement officer or social services worker may take the child into temporary physical custody immediately, without a court order. Within twelve hours after taking a child into custody (twenty-four hours if any of the first twelve-hour period falls on a weekend or holiday), the social services department must either (1) file a petition and obtain a court order or (2) return the child to the parent.

Juvenile court procedures that follow the filing of a petition are discussed in Chapter 13.

Protective Services

After determining that a child is an abused, neglected, or dependent juvenile, the social services department must evaluate the need for protective services and develop a plan for protecting the child and working with the family.[42]

Protective services help parents (or guardians, custodians, or caretakers)

* prevent abuse or neglect,
* improve the quality of child care,
* be better parents or care providers, and
* preserve and stabilize family life.[43]

Subject to the exceptions described above, the director can continue to demand confidential information that would assist at this stage of providing protective services, just as during an assessment.[44]

If the department has not filed a petition to start a juvenile court action in order to obtain a nonsecure custody order, the department must file one at any point at which it believes that the child should be removed from the home or that the court needs to become involved for any other reason.

Keeping the Family Together

State law and policy reflect the belief that children who can remain safely in their own homes or return safely to their own homes after removal almost always are better off than they would be in foster care or other substitute care arrangements. Law and policy also reflect parents' rights to the care, custody, and control of their children—rights the parents may relinquish through conduct that is inconsistent with their protected parental status. Even when abuse or neglect has occurred, the law requires county departments of social services to make reasonable efforts to keep the family together. Originally the phrase "reasonable efforts" referred to a county department of social services' diligent use of services (1) to prevent the need to remove a child from the home or, (2) if a child had been removed from the home, to return the child home.[45]

The current definition reflects an additional belief—that children need stable, permanent homes and are harmed by delays in achieving that goal. Now, if a court determines that the child's remaining at home or returning home is not consistent with achieving a safe permanent home for the child in a reasonable period of time, "reasonable efforts" also refers to a social services department's diligent use of permanency planning services to develop and implement another permanent plan for a child.[46] The requirement that social services departments make these efforts is both a funding condition for the state's receipt of federal child welfare funds and a mandate of state law.[47]

Any juvenile court order that places or continues the placement of a child in the custody of a department of social services must include findings about whether the department has made reasonable efforts. Depending on prior actions in the case, the findings must relate to efforts to prevent the need for placement, to reunify the child and parents, or to achieve another permanent plan.[48] If the child is in social services' custody, the court must make these findings at

- hearings on the need for continued prehearing (nonsecure) custody,
- disposition hearings, and
- review and permanency planning hearings (see Chapter 13).[49]

In these orders, the court also may provide for services or other efforts aimed at returning the child to a safe home or achieving another permanent plan for the child.

When a child needs placement because of an immediate threat of harm, the court can determine later that it was reasonable for the social services department to place the child without making any efforts to prevent the need for placement.[50] If the court finds that a department of social services has not made reasonable efforts to prevent or eliminate the need for a child's placement, the court still may enter whatever order is appropriate. For example, even if social services has provided no services to help a parent find decent housing, when unsafe living conditions are the reason for the child's removal, the court may continue the child's placement outside the home. However, the negative finding may prevent social services from claiming federal funds to pay part of the cost of the child's foster care placement.[51]

Making reasonable efforts to prevent or eliminate the need for a child's placement does not mean making every possible effort, and it does not mean making efforts for an indefinite period of time. Parents are responsible for providing a safe home for their children and for correcting the conditions that led to a child's removal from the parents' custody. The court may relieve a social services department of the duty to make efforts to reunify the family if the court finds any of the following:

1. The efforts clearly would be futile.
2. The efforts would be inconsistent with the child's health, safety, and need for a safe, permanent home within a reasonable period of time.

3. The parent's rights to another child have been terminated involuntarily by a court.
4. A court has determined that the parent has
   - committed murder or voluntary manslaughter of another child of the parent;
   - aided, abetted, attempted, conspired, or solicited to commit murder or voluntary manslaughter of the child or another child of the parent;
   - committed a felony assault resulting in serious bodily injury to the child or another child of the parent;
   - committed sexual abuse against the child or another child of the parent; or
   - been required to register as a sex offender on any government-administered registry.[52]

After the court has ordered that reunification efforts cease, the emphasis in the case shifts. The social services department still must make reasonable efforts, but those efforts are directed toward developing and implementing another permanent plan for the child. That plan might be adoption or the designation of a relative or other appropriate person as the child's guardian or legal custodian.

A parent who fails to make the changes necessary to provide a safe home for the child within a reasonable period of time risks permanent separation from the child. The court may terminate a parent's rights completely—freeing the child for adoption—if the court finds that the parent has willfully left the child in foster care or other out-of-home placement for more than a year without making reasonable progress in correcting the conditions that led to the child's removal from the home.[53]

Notification Requirements at Conclusion of Assessment
To the Reporter
Within five working days after completing an assessment, the department of social services must give the person who made the report a second written notice, unless the reporter asked not to be notified or did not identify himself or herself. (The first notice will have informed the reporter that the

report was accepted for assessment. See "Notifying the Reporter," above.) This notice must state

1. whether the department has made a finding of abuse, neglect, or dependency;
2. whether the department is taking action to protect the child and, if so, what that action is;
3. whether the department has filed a petition to begin a juvenile court proceeding;
4. that if the reporter is not satisfied with the director's decision, then within five working days after receiving the notice, the reporter may ask the prosecutor (the assistant district attorney who handles juvenile cases) to review the decision; and
5. the procedure for requesting a formal review by the prosecutor (see Chapter 12).[54]

Because of confidentiality requirements, the department ordinarily cannot share much more information than this with the reporter.

To the Parent, Guardian, Custodian, or Caretaker

If an assessment does not result in a finding of abuse, neglect, or dependency, the social services director must notify those listed below of that result and inform them that social services will no longer be involved with the family on a non-voluntary basis:

- any person who was alleged to have abused or neglected the child;
- any parent or other person with whom the child resided when social services began the assessment; and
- any agency that has legal custody of the child.[55]

If the assessment does result in a finding of abuse, neglect, or dependency, the social worker in the case must "make every effort to provide personal written notice" to the same people or agencies.[56]

To the Central Registry

Each county department of social services must furnish the state Department of Health and Human Services with data about abuse and neglect reports and assessments (as well as dependency and child death reports and assessments). At the state level, this comprehensive collection of information from across the state is called the Central Registry.[57] Created in 1971, the registry provides data for studying the nature and extent of child abuse, neglect, dependency, and fatalities caused by maltreatment in North Carolina. It also helps identify children and families who are involved in repeated reports or instances of these occurrences.

Registry data are confidential. State rules specify the circumstances in which the data can be used for research and study and when the Chief Medical Examiner's office and law enforcement officials may use the data to determine whether abuse or neglect should be evaluated as a possible factor in a child's death.[58] The Juvenile Code does not provide any procedure for a parent, guardian, custodian, or caretaker to contest a social services department's determination at the end of an assessment or to request the removal of information from the Central Registry. For that reason, information in the registry is not available to prospective employers or to anyone else who is conducting a background check of an individual.

To a Responsible Individual and the Responsible Individuals List

In some cases, after completing an investigative assessment, the social services department is required to give personal written notice (or, if that is not possible, notice by registered or certified mail) to someone the department has identified as being responsible for the abuse or serious neglect of a child.[59] The department also must furnish that information to the state Department of Health and Human Services.

The focus of the reporting law, child protective services, and juvenile court proceedings is on children who are abused, neglected, or dependent and their need for protection, services, or placement.[60] However, if a social services department determines that a child has been abused or seriously neglected, the department is also required, when possible, to identify the individual or individuals responsible for the child's being abused or neglected.[61] These people's names may end up on a state-maintained list from which information can be disclosed to

- child caring institutions,
- child placing agencies,
- group home facilities, and
- other providers of foster care, child care, or adoption services who need to determine an individual's fitness to care for or adopt children.[62]

Because information from the Responsible Individuals List can be disclosed and could substantially impact an individual's reputation and opportunities to adopt or care for children, a person has a right to contest the placement of his or her name on the list. The first statutory procedures provided for this kind of challenge were declared unconstitutional because they allowed immediate placement of names on the list and required people to seek expunction of their names from the list.[63] The current procedures permit placement of a name on the list only after the identified person has had an opportunity to challenge social services' determination that it should go there or the person has been criminally convicted as a result of the same incident that led to the assessment.[64] These procedures were created by legislation that became effective July 3, 2010, and the only names on the list now are those placed there pursuant to these procedures.[65]

The term "serious neglect" is relevant only in relation to

1. a social services department's determination of whether the appropriate response to a report is a family assessment or an investigative assessment, and
2. a social services department's or court's determination of whether someone is a "responsible individual."[66]

Children are not adjudicated by the court to be seriously neglected. The definition of "serious neglect" suggests that a social services department must exercise substantial discretion in making the initial determination that someone is a responsible individual based on having seriously neglected a child. Serious neglect is "[c]onduct, behavior, or inaction of the juvenile's parent, guardian, custodian, or caretaker that evidences a disregard of consequences of such magnitude that the conduct, behavior, or inaction constitutes an unequivocal danger to the juvenile's health, welfare, or safety, but does not constitute abuse."[67]

To the State Department of Health and Human Services and the State Bureau of Investigation When a Child Care Facility Is Involved

If an assessment reveals evidence that a child has been abused or neglected in a child care facility, the social services director must immediately notify the state Department of Health and Human Services (DHHS) and, if the evidence relates to sexual abuse in a child care facility, the State Bureau of Investigation (SBI).[68] Child care facilities include child care centers and family child care homes, which are regulated by the state.[69] At the conclusion of the assessment, the social services director must follow up with written notice of the results of the assessment to DHHS and, if the assessment related to sexual abuse in a child care facility, to the SBI.[70]

Confidentiality and Information Sharing
Confidentiality Rule

A county social services department is required to hold "in strictest confidence" the information it receives in relation to a child protective services matter, including the identity of the reporter.[71] The department also must protect information in its records about children who are in the department's custody[72] and information that would reveal the identity of any juvenile who is the subject of a report or assessment.[73] Except when disclosure is for purposes directly related to the administration of a social services program or is explicitly authorized by a statute or regulation, it is a misdemeanor for anyone to disclose (or, for that matter, to obtain) information concerning persons who are receiving social services when the information is derived from the department's records, files, or communications.[74]

When Disclosure Is Allowed

Information in the agency's child protective services records can be disclosed any time a court orders the social services director to disclose it. Without a court order, information from social services' records in a child protective services case may be disclosed

- to a federal, state, or local government agency that needs the information in order to protect a child from abuse or neglect or to carry out its mandated responsibilities;
- to the child, even if the child is eighteen or older, or the child's attorney or guardian ad litem;
- to individuals or agencies that are helping provide or facilitate the provision of services to the child;
- to a district attorney who needs access to the information to carry out his or her responsibilities relating to a report of abuse or a director's decision not to file a petition; and

- to the other parties in a juvenile court proceeding involving the child, when the information is relevant to that proceeding and does not include the identity of the person who made a report to social services.[75]

In addition, throughout the life of the case—from the assessment stage through any court action that may occur—certain agencies must share with each other information that is relevant to the case, but they may use the information only

- for the child's protection,
- for the protection of others, or
- to improve the child's educational opportunities.[76]

Agencies covered by this requirement are designated in a rule issued by the Division of Juvenile Justice in the Department of Public Safety and include the following:

1. the Division of Juvenile Justice of the Department of Public Safety;
2. the Office of Guardian Ad Litem Services of the Administrative Office of the Courts;
3. county departments of social services;
4. area mental health, developmental disability, and substance abuse authorities;
5. local law enforcement agencies;
6. district attorneys' offices, although they are never required to disclose information pursuant to the rule;
7. county mental health facilities and developmental disabilities and substance abuse programs;
8. local school administrative units;
9. local health departments; and
10. any local agency designated by an administrative order issued by the chief district court judge of the district in which the agency is located.[77]

Any confidential information shared by these designated agencies must remain confidential and be withheld from public inspection.[78] If one agency refuses another agency's request for information for any reason, the agency refusing to disclose information must inform the other agency of the specific law or regulation that is the basis for the refusal.[79]

Defining appropriate boundaries for the sharing of information about children and families involved in the juvenile court and social services systems is not easy. Even with the legal and regulatory guidance described here, the exact boundaries are sometimes unclear.[80] The applicable law and rules are likely to be the subject of continued scrutiny and of efforts to reconcile competing interests such as

- the need to share sensitive information in order for agencies and professionals to serve families effectively and to coordinate their involvement with families,
- the desire to respect families' and children's privacy,
- an interest in not having fear of publicity and loss of privacy discourage people from involvement in the system,
- the public's interest in knowing how well the child protective services system works and in feeling that it is accountable, and
- the need to comply with federal and state confidentiality laws and regulations that often are difficult to interpret or reconcile.

Local guidelines or protocols among agencies can help clarify when, how, and with whom certain kinds of information can be shared and for what purposes the information may be used. They also can help ensure that the person or agency receiving confidential information continues to protect its confidentiality.

Notes

1. *See* North Carolina General Statutes (hereinafter G.S.) § 7B-101(1), (9), and (15). The North Carolina General Statutes can be viewed online at www.ncga.state.nc.us/gascripts/Statutes/StatutesTOC.pl.

2. Even if the eighteen-year-old was disabled and dependent on her parents for care, the report would be screened out as a child abuse or neglect report. It would be treated as a report under the Protection of the Abused, Neglected or Exploited Disabled Adult Act (G.S. Chapter 108A, Article 6), which also includes a mandatory reporting requirement. The person making the report would be referred to the department's adult protective services unit.

3. The department would relay the information to law enforcement authorities as required by G.S. 7B-307(a). In addition, physicians and hospitals have a duty to report to law enforcement cases involving "serious physical injury to any child under the age of 18 years where the . . . injury appears, in the physician's professional judgment, to be the result of nonaccidental trauma." G.S. 90-21.20(c1).

4. G.S. 7B-307(a).

5. Administrative rules relating to child protective services appear in subchapter 70A of title 10A of the North Carolina Administrative Code (hereinafter N.C.A.C.).

6. Policies relating to child protective services appear in N.C. Department of Health & Human Services, Division of Social Services, Chapter VIII, of the Division's online *Family Support and Child Welfare Manual* (hereinafter *State Manual*), http://info.dhhs.state.nc.us/olm/manuals/dss/csm-60/man.

7. *See* "Structured Intake," *in* Section 1407, Chapter VIII, *State Manual*, cited in full in note 6.

8. N.C.A.C. tit. 10A, subch. 70A, § .0105(g) (Apr. 2003).

9. G.S. 7B-302(f).

10. N.C.A.C. tit. 10A, subch. 70A, § .0105(h) (Apr. 2003).

11. *See* G.S. 7B-307(a).

12. *See id.*

13. *See id.*

14. G.S. 7B-301.

15. G.S. 7B-301(c), as amended by S.L. 2013-52, sec. 7, effective December 1, 2013.

16. G.S. 7B-302; N.C.A.C. tit. 10A, subch. 70A, § .0106 (Apr. 2003).

17. G.S. 7B-101(11a) and (11b). The Multiple Response System involves much more than the two kinds of assessment responses mentioned in the text. It represents an "on-going effort to reform the entire continuum of child welfare services" and comprises seven key strategies as part of that effort. *See* "Multiple Response System," *in* Section 1400.III, Chapter VIII, *State Manual*, cited in full in note 6, http://info.dhhs.state.nc.us/olm/manuals/dss/csm-60/man/CS1400-02.htm#TopOfPage. Additional information about the Multiple Response System is available on the web page of the state Division of Social Services, www.ncdhhs.gov/dss/mrs/#what.

18. N.C.A.C. tit. 10A, subch. 70A, § .0103(a) (Sept. 1994).

19. N.C.A.C. tit. 10A, subch. 70A, § .0103(b) (Sept. 1994). Policies and procedures applicable to cases involving more than one county are discussed in Chapter V (Jurisdiction in Child Welfare), *State Manual*, cited in full in note 6, http://info.dhhs.state.nc.us/olm/manuals/dss/csm-45/man/Chapter_V-02.htm#P409_36256.

20. G.S. 7B-302(a).

21. G.S. 7B-302(a); N.C.A.C. tit. 10A, subch. 70A, § .0105(d) (Apr. 2003).

22. G.S. 7B-302(a).

23. G.S. 7B-302(h).

24. G.S. 7B-302(e).

25. G.S. 15A-285. The statutory authority for this type of entry may not be used as the basis for law enforcement action taken to enforce the law or seize a person or evidence. *Id.*

26. N.C.A.C. tit. 10A, subch. 70A, § .0105(d) (Apr. 2003). *See also* Section 1408.III.E.3, Chapter VIII, *State Manual*, cited in full in note 6, http://info.dhhs.state.nc.us/olm/manuals/dss/csm-60/man/CS1408-01.htm#P164_16882.

27. N.C.A.C. tit. 10A, subch. 70A, § .0106 (Apr. 2003).

28. *See* Section 1408.II.J, Chapter VIII, *State Manual*, cited in full in note 6, http://info.dhhs.state.nc.us/olm/manuals/dss/csm-60/man/CS1408-01.htm#P681_74129.

29. *See* Section 1408.III.E, Chapter VIII, *State Manual*, cited in full in note 6, http://info.dhhs.state.nc.us/olm/manuals/dss/csm-60/man/CS1408-02.htm#P921_98338, and Section 1408.IV.F, Chapter VIII, *State Manual*, cited in full in note 6, http://info.dhhs.state.nc.us/olm/manuals/dss/csm-60/man/CS1408-03.htm#P1047_118651.

30. *See* G.S. 7B-101(1), (9), and (15).

31. If a social services department takes a case to court, it has the burden of proving by "clear and convincing evidence" that the child is abused, neglected, or dependent. G.S. 7B-805. Arguably, a department should not substantiate a report unless it believes it could satisfy that burden if the case goes to court.

32. *See* Section 1408.III.E, Chapter VIII, *State Manual*, cited in full in note 6, http://info.dhhs.state.nc.us/olm/manuals/dss/csm-60/man/CS1408-02.htm#P921_98338.

33. G.S. 7B-302(e).

34. Federal laws and regulations that prohibit disclosure of information include the Family Educational Rights and Privacy Act (FERPA) (20 U.S.C. § 1232g; 34 C.F.R. Part 99), which protects the privacy of student education records, and the Public Health Service Act (42 U.S.C. § 290dd-2; 42 C.F.R. Part 2), which restricts the disclosure of drug and alcohol abuse patient records. These restrictions do not apply to reporting suspected child abuse under state reporting laws, but they appear to apply at any stage after reporting, i.e., during an assessment or the provision of protective services. For additional information about these and other confidential records, see Kella W. Hatcher, Janet Mason, and John Rubin, *Abuse, Neglect, Dependency, and Termination of Parental Rights Proceedings in North Carolina* (Chapel Hill, N.C.: UNC School of Government, 2011) (hereinafter *Abuse, Neglect, Dependency, and Termination of Parental Rights Proceedings*), Sections 13.4 and 13.5, available for purchase or for free download, in PDF form, at http://shopping.netsuite.com/s.nl/c.433425/it.A/id.4228/.f.

35. G.S. 7B-302(e).

36. *Id.*

37. G.S. 7B-302(b).

38. *Id.*

39. G.S. 7B-302(e).

40. G.S. 7B-307(a).

41. *Id.*

42. N.C.A.C. tit. 10A, subch. 70A, §§ .0107(c), (d) (May 2006).

43. G.S. 7B-300.

44. G.S. 7B-302(e). See also G.S. 7B-3100(a), which requires that certain designated agencies share information that is "relevant to . . . the provision or arrangement of protective services in a child abuse, neglect, or dependency case." Note that the administrative rules issued pursuant to that statute, at N.C.A.C. tit. 28, subch. 01A, §§ .0301 and .0302 (Apr. 2003), have not been amended to reflect the expansion of the statutory provision to include social services' provision of protective services as well as its assessment of a report of abuse, neglect, or dependency.

45. These requirements were first articulated in the Adoption Assistance and Child Welfare Act of 1980, Public Law 96-272, which amended the Social Security Act, 42 U.S.C. §§ 601 *et seq.*

46. The definition of "reasonable efforts" is found in G.S. 7B-101(18).

47. *See* 42 U.S.C. § 671 and G.S. 7B-507.

48. G.S. 7B-507(a).

49. G.S. 7B-507(c). These requirements also apply in cases of delinquent or undisciplined juveniles who are placed by the court in the custody of a county department of social services. *See* G.S. 7B-2503(1)c and 7B-2506(1)c.

50. G.S. 7B-507(a).

51. *See* Section 13.1B in Hatcher, Mason, and Rubin, *Abuse, Neglect, Dependency, and Termination of Parental Rights Proceedings*, cited in full in note 34.

52. G.S. 7B-507(b).

53. G.S. 7B-1111(a)(2). This is just one of the statutory grounds for terminating a parent's rights. Termination of parental rights is discussed in detail in Chapter 9 of Hatcher, Mason, and Rubin, *Abuse, Neglect, Dependency, and Termination of Parental Rights*, cited in full in note 34.

54. G.S. 7B-302(g).

55. N.C.A.C. tit. 10A, subch. 70A, § .0108 (July 1993). The rule does not specify the form or timing of this notification.

56. N.C.A.C. tit. 10A, subch. 70A, § .0107 (May 2006).

57. G.S. 7B-311; G.S. 7B-307(c).

58. N.C.A.C. tit. 10A, subch. 70A, § .0102 (May 2006).

59. G.S. 7B-320(a), (b). The statute describes the required content of the written notification. G.S. 7B-320(c).

60. *See, e.g., In re* S.C.R., ___ N.C. App. ___, 718 S.E.2d 709, 713 (2011) (holding that the trial court should not have dismissed the petition as to the father because an adjudication of abuse, neglect, or dependency pertains to the status of the child and not to the identity of any perpetrator of abuse or neglect of the child).

61. G.S. 7B-302 and -307.

62. G.S. 7B-311(b) and -320(c)(3).

63. *See In re* W.B.M., 202 N.C. App. 606, 690 S.E.2d 41 (2010).

64. G.S. 7B-311.

65. S.L. 2010-90. Current statutes relating to the Responsible Individuals List include G.S. 7B-101(18a) and (19a); 7B-311; and 7B-320, -323, and -324. For more detailed information about the Responsible Individuals List and related procedures, see "Responsible Individuals List," *in* Section 1427, Chapter VIII, *State Manual*, cited in full in note 6, http://info.dhhs.state.nc.us/olm/manuals/dss/csm-60/man/CS1427.htm#TopOfPage.

66. *See* G.S. 7B-101(18a), -320(a), -323(d).

67. G.S. 7B-101(19a).

68. G.S. 7B-307(b). Effective December 1, 2013, a social services director who receives a report of sexual abuse of a child in a child care facility and knowingly fails to notify the State Bureau of Investigation is guilty of a Class 1 misdemeanor. S.L. 2013-52, sec. 7, added this provision as G.S. 7B-301(c).

69. The terms "child care center" and "family child care home" are defined in G.S. 110-86(3). For provisions relating to the authority of the state Department of

Health and Human Services to investigate reports of child abuse or neglect in child care settings and to impose administrative sanctions, see N.C.A.C. tit. 9, §§ .1901 and .2213(b) (Apr. 2001).

70. G.S. 7B-307(c).

71. G.S. 7B-302(a1).

72. G.S. 7B-2901(b).

73. G.S. 7B-3100(b).

74. G.S. 108A-80.

75. G.S. 7B-302(a1) and -700(a); N.C.A.C. tit. 10A, subch. 70A, § .0113 (Sept. 1991).

76. G.S. 7B-3100(a). The sharing of school information must be in accordance with the Family Educational Rights and Privacy Act (FERPA), 20 U.S.C. § 1232g.

77. N.C.A.C. tit. 28, subch. 01A, § .0301 (Apr. 2003).

78. N.C.A.C. tit. 28, subch. 01A, § .0302 (Apr. 2003).

79. N.C.A.C. tit. 28, subch. 01A, § .0302(b) (Apr. 2003).

80. For an excellent discussion of confidentiality concepts and issues, see John L. Saxon, "Confidentiality and Social Services (Part I): What Is Confidentiality?" *Social Services Law Bulletin* No. 30 (Feb. 2001); "Confidentiality and Social Services (Part II): Where Do Confidentiality Rules Come From?" *Social Services Law Bulletin* No. 31 (May 2001); "Confidentiality and Social Services (Part III): A Process for Analyzing Issues Involving Confidentiality," *Social Services Law Bulletin* No. 35 (Apr. 2002); "Confidentiality and Social Services (Part IV): An Annotated Index of Federal and State Confidentiality Laws," *Social Services Law Bulletin* No. 37 (Oct. 2002). Each of these articles may be downloaded, in PDF form, at no charge, at http://shopping.netsuite.com/s.nl/c.433425/sc.7/category.64/.f. For further information, call the School of Government Bookstore at 919.966.4119.

Chapter 12

Review Procedures

Review of Decision to Screen Out a Report

A person whose report to a county department of social services is *screened out* (that is, not accepted for assessment) is entitled to an agency review of the department's decision. (See "Notification after a Report Is Made" in Chapter 11.) For example, if a principal reports that a nine-year-old child has excessive absences from school, a county social services department may decline to accept the report or to conduct an assessment on the ground that the situation, even if exactly as described by the principal, does not constitute neglect. If the principal disagrees and thinks that the child's absences are due to a lack of proper care and supervision by the child's parents (a form of neglect), the principal may request a review of the department's decision. In most cases the principal first would talk informally with a social worker, a supervisor, or the director of the department of social services.

Each county department of social services must establish a process for conducting agency reviews of decisions to screen out reports when the person who made the report requests an agency review. At a minimum, each department's process must include

1. notifying the reporter of the basis for the department's decision and of the reporter's right to and the procedures for obtaining a review of the decision,
2. designating the persons within the agency who will conduct the reviews, and
3. specifying the manner in which the reviews will be conducted.[1]

There is no provision for further review of a decision to screen out a report.

Informal Review of Department's Determination after an Assessment

If the department of social services accepts a report and the person who made it is not satisfied with the outcome of the department's assessment, that person may communicate directly with the social worker handling the case. Sometimes the social worker can provide information about the department's actions that will dispel the reporter's dissatisfaction with the department's response. (Of course, confidentiality may limit the department's ability to give full details of the assessment. See Chapter 11.) Or the social worker may be able to explain legal or other constraints of which the reporter was unaware. Likewise, the reporter may be able to give the social worker additional information or a perspective that would lead the department to rethink its response.

If this kind of communication does not resolve the reporter's dissatisfaction, the reporter may contact the following persons, preferably in this order:

1. the social worker's supervisor,
2. the head of the child protective services unit in the agency, or
3. the county director of social services.

Neither the county social services board nor any individual board member has a role in relation to an individual case decision. (See "County Social Services Boards," below.)

Formal Review of Case Decisions

In most cases, even if the department determines after an assessment that a child is abused, neglected, or dependent, the department does not file a petition to take the matter to juvenile court. Instead, it provides protective services and develops with the family a plan aimed at ensuring the child's safety and well-being. A reporter who disagrees with the department's decision not to file a petition has a right to ask the local prosecutor to review that decision.[2]

The statute refers to the review in relation to the social services director's decision not to file a petition in juvenile court. The review clearly is available when the social services department makes a finding of abuse, neglect, or dependency but does not file a petition. It is not as clear whether it is available when the department, after an assessment, does not make a finding of any of those conditions and therefore obviously is not filing a petition. If review by the prosecutor is not available in that circumstance, the Juvenile Code provides no formal procedure for questioning the adequacy of the department's assessment or the correctness of its determination. The informal procedures described above, of course, would be available.

Requests for prosecutors to review case decisions are not made frequently, but they are the only formal recourse for someone who is dissatisfied with the social services department's response to a report following an assessment. If informal steps do not seem effective, this process for external review is an important alternative for someone who knows or strongly suspects that a child is abused, neglected, or dependent and feels that the department's response is inadequate.

Requesting Formal Review

The reporter may request a review by the prosecutor within five working days after receiving the second written notice from the department of social services.[3] That is the notice that tells the reporter the outcome of the assessment (including whether the department has filed a petition to take the matter to court) and explains the procedures for requesting a review of a decision not to file a petition.[4] Presumably, if the department does not give the reporter the second written notice as required, the time within which the reporter can request a review is extended to at least five days following the date the reporter learns of the department's decision. Someone who asks to be notified orally rather than in writing probably has five days after the oral notification to request a review. A reporter who does not identify himself or herself or who asks not to be notified of the outcome of the assessment effectively waives his or her right to request a review. These situations are not specifically addressed by either the statute or the administrative rules.

Timing of Review

When the person who made a report requests a review of the department's decision not to file a petition, the prosecutor must notify that person and the social services director of the time and place for the review. The prosecutor must conduct the review within twenty days after the reporter receives notice of the department's decision not to file a petition.[5]

Review Process and Conclusion

In conducting a review, the prosecutor should confer with the person who made the report, the protective services social worker, the child (if that is practicable), and anyone else who has pertinent information about the child or the child's family.[6]

After the review, the prosecutor may

1. affirm the social services director's decision,
2. ask a local law enforcement agency to investigate the allegations in the report, or
3. direct the social services director to file a petition in juvenile court.[7]

Review of Agency Practices or Community Issues

The informal channels for reviewing case decisions described above also may be appropriate when an individual, a group, an agency, or an institution has concerns about a social services department's general practices or policies regarding child protective services. Anyone who is concerned about agency practices, or about broader community issues involving child protection, should consult first with the county social services director if that is feasible. Concerns also may be taken to the state Division of Social Services, the county social services board (or its equivalent), or the local community child protection team described below.

County Social Services Boards

Most counties have a three- or five-member county social services board.[8] This board's responsibilities include

- hiring the county social services director,
- consulting with the director about problems relating to the director's office,
- helping the director plan the department's budget, and
- advising local authorities about policies and plans to improve social conditions in the community.[9]

The county board of social services does not have a role in making or reviewing decisions in individual cases involving child protective services. However, the board should have a strong interest in the adequacy of the department's child protective services program in general (including its funding), the public's understanding of that program, and the larger community's response to the problems of child abuse and neglect in the county.[10]

State Division of Social Services

Although child protective services programs are administered by the counties, the state also has a role.[11] The Division of Social Services (the Division) in the state Department of Health and Human Services (DHHS) provides county social services departments with

- training, consultation, and technical assistance;
- policy manuals that serve as the day-to-day guide for county social services staff;[12] and
- regular periodic program reviews.[13]

The Division's staff includes children's program representatives who work with designated groups of counties and are available for consultation on issues of policy and practice in child welfare cases.[14] In addition, four assistant attorneys general specializing in child welfare law work with the Division to provide training, consultation, and legal assistance to the county departments. Inquiries about child welfare can be made to the DHHS Customer Service Center or directly to the Division's Raleigh office.[15]

The Department of Health and Human Services has statutory authority to intervene if a county social services department fails to provide child protective services in accordance with state law and regulations or fails to show reasonable efforts to do so.[16] The ultimate intervention, which has never occurred, would be the state's taking over operation of the county program based on a finding that the county's failures posed "a substantial threat to the safety and welfare of children in the county" who receive or are eligible for services.[17]

Community Child Protection Teams

Every county has an interdisciplinary community child protection team that reviews selected child protective services cases.[18] All teams review child fatality cases in which a child's death is suspected to have resulted from abuse or neglect and

1. a report about the child or the child's family was made to social services within the preceding twelve months, or

2. the child or the child's family received child welfare services within twelve months of the child's death.[19]

Each team can define other categories of cases it wishes to review.[20] In addition, the county social services director may bring cases to the team for review, and any team member may request review of a specific case.[21]

These reviews are not appeals. They are designed to help the team fulfill its broader goals of

- developing a community-wide approach to problems of child abuse and neglect;
- understanding the causes of childhood deaths;
- identifying any gaps or deficiencies in the delivery of services to children and families; and
- making and implementing recommendations for changes to laws, rules, and policies that will support children's safe and healthy development and prevent child abuse and neglect.[22]

The team makes recommendations to the board of county commissioners and promotes agency collaboration to create or improve community resources for children.[23]

The law provides for each local community child protection team to include

- the county social services director and a member of the social services staff,
- a local law enforcement officer,
- an attorney from the district attorney's office,
- a representative of the local community action agency,
- the superintendent or other representative of each local school administrative unit,
- a member of the county social services board,
- a local mental health professional,
- a representative of the local guardian ad litem program,
- the director of the local public health department, and
- a local health care provider.[24]

The board of county commissioners may appoint up to five additional team members. Each local team elects its own chair and meets at least four times a year.

Since information about particular cases is confidential, the parts of team meetings devoted to reviewing individual cases are not open to the public. Parts of the meetings that do not involve confidential information—for example, discussions of general findings, recommendations, or community needs—should be open to the public. Information about a county's community child protection team can be obtained from the county manager's office, from one of the agencies represented on the team, or from the state Division of Social Services, which provides coordination for the community child protection team program.

Notes

1. N.C. Admin. Code (hereinafter N.C.A.C.) tit. 10A, subch. 70A, § .0105(h) (Apr. 2003).

2. North Carolina General Statutes (hereinafter G.S.) § 7B-305. "Prosecutor" refers to the district attorney or an assistant district attorney assigned by the district attorney to handle cases in juvenile court. G.S. 7B-101(17). The North Carolina General Statutes can be viewed online at www.ncga.state.nc.us/gascripts/Statutes/StatutesTOC.pl.

3. G.S. 7B-302(g). *See also* N.C.A.C. tit. 10A, subch. 70A, § 0109 (Sept. 1994).

4. G.S. 7B-302(g).

5. G.S. 7B-306; N.C.A.C. tit. 10A, subch. 70A, § .0109 (Sept. 1994).

6. G.S. 7B-306.

7. *Id.*

8. In those counties the board of county commissioners and the state Social Services Commission each appoint one or two members of the county social services board, and those members appoint the third or fifth member. *See* G.S. 108A-2. For many years Mecklenburg County and Wake County have operated consolidated human services agencies pursuant to G.S. 153A-77, which allowed boards of county commissioners in counties with a population of 425,000 or more to abolish their social services boards and either assume the powers and duties of the board or establish a consolidated human services board. Effective June 29, 2012, those options became available to boards of county commissioners in every county, regardless of population size. *See* S.L. 2012-126. Several counties have exercised those options and others may follow. *See* Aimee Wall, "Recent Developments in Organization and Governance of Local Human Services Agencies," *Coates' Canons: NC Local Government Law Blog*, September 25, 2012, http://canons.sog.unc.edu/?p=6853, and Aimee Wall, "Organization and Governance of Social Services: New Options for Counties," *Coates' Canons: NC Local Government Law Blog*, August 10, 2012, http://canons.sog.unc.edu/?p=6798.

9. G.S 108A-9. *See also* John L. Saxon, *Handbook for County Social Services Boards* (Chapel Hill, N.C.: UNC School of Government, 2009).

10. County social services boards meet monthly, and their meetings are open to the public. To learn when and where a board meets or how to contact the board

chairperson, call the county department of social services. Contact information for county social services departments can be found at www.ncdhhs.gov/dss/local.

11. In most states, the state administers social services programs. In North Carolina, the counties perform that role with some oversight by the state. For a description of the social services system in North Carolina, see John L. Saxon, *Social Services in North Carolina* (Chapel Hill, N.C.: UNC School of Government, 2008).

12. The manuals are available at http://info.dhhs.state.nc.us/olm/manuals/manuals.aspx?dc=dss.

13. The Division of Social Services conducts regular Child and Family Services Reviews of each county's children's services program. The review protocol and related information about the reviews are available at www.ncdhhs.gov/dss/stats/cw.htm.

14. Contact information for the children's program representatives and the counties to which they are assigned can be found at www.ncdhhs.gov/dss/team/CPRList.html.

15. The main number for the State Division of Social Services is 919.733.3055. The number for Child Welfare Customer Service at the Division is 919.733.9467. Additional contact information is available at www.ncdhhs.gov/dss/contact.

16. G.S. 108A-74.

17. G.S. 108A-74(c). In this eventuality, the county director of social services "shall be divested of all service delivery powers conferred upon [him or her]." *Id.*

18. Statutory provisions relating to community child protection teams and the North Carolina Child Fatality Task Force are located in Article 14 of G.S. Chapter 7B (G.S. 7B-1400 through -1414).

19. G.S. 7B-1406(a)(1).

20. G.S. 7B-1406(a)(2).

21. G.S. 7B-1409.

22. N.C.A.C. tit. 10A, subch. 70A, § .0201 (Sept. 1994).

23. G.S. 7B-1406(a)(2); N.C.A.C. tit. 10A, subch. 70A, § .0201 (Sept. 1994).

24. G.S. 7B-1407(a), (b). Either this team or a separate child fatality prevention team also reviews additional child fatalities in the county. A community child protection team that also reviews additional child fatalities must include an emergency medical services provider or firefighter, a district court judge, a county medical examiner, a representative of a local child care facility or Head Start program, and a parent of a child who died before age eighteen. G.S. 7B-1407(c).

Chapter 13

Juvenile Court Procedures

The procedures described in this chapter are those set out in the North Carolina Juvenile Code (the Code).[1] Other laws and different procedures apply to proceedings for adoption, voluntary admissions and involuntary commitments of minors to mental health treatment facilities, and custody disputes between parents.[2]

Abuse, Neglect, or Dependency Petition

Sometimes, when an assessment results in a finding of abuse, neglect, or dependency, protective services cannot protect the child adequately unless the child is removed from the home. And sometimes, the parent (or guardian, custodian, or caretaker) refuses to accept services that are needed to ensure the child's safety. In these situations, the social services director must sign and file a petition alleging the relevant facts; alleging that the child is abused, neglected, or dependent; and asking the court to intervene on the child's behalf. The filing of a petition begins a juvenile proceeding in the district court. Only a county director of social services (or the director's representative) can file an abuse, neglect, or dependency petition.[3]

Juvenile proceedings are civil actions (that is, they are not criminal prosecutions). They focus on the condition and needs of the child, not the guilt or innocence of the parent or anyone else. County departments of social services file petitions in only a small percentage of the cases in which they determine that a child is abused, neglected, or dependent. Usually this is because

- the department's assessment indicates that it is safe for the child to remain in the home,
- the family accepts services voluntarily,
- the family and the department agree on a "protection plan" that provides for the family to take steps to protect the child or to voluntarily place the child with a relative, or
- the person who abused or neglected the child is out of the home and the child is no longer at risk.

Prehearing Custody

The Juvenile Code term for a prehearing custody order is "nonsecure custody." The Code uses this somewhat confusing term in order to distinguish foster care and similar placements from the detention ("secure custody") of children who are alleged to be delinquent. When the social services department determines after an assessment that a child is abused, neglected, or dependent and files a petition in juvenile court, it often asks for a prehearing custody order authorizing the department to place the child immediately in foster care (or another appropriate setting) without waiting for a full hearing on the petition.[4]

When the custody order is sought, a social services worker or law enforcement officer may already have taken the child into custody without a court order. They are allowed to do this if the child might be harmed or disappear if they attempted to file a petition and get the court order before taking custody of the child. To keep the child longer than twelve hours (or twenty-four hours if a weekend or holiday is involved), the social services department must file a petition and get a custody order within that time. (See "Immediate Removal of Child" in Chapter 11.)

Before granting a request for a prehearing custody order, a judge must consider releasing the child to a parent or another responsible adult. If that is not possible, then to grant the order the judge must find that there is a "reasonable factual basis" for believing that

1. the facts alleged in the petition are true,
2. removing the child from the home is the only reasonable way to protect the child, and
3. one of the following is true:
   - the child has been abandoned;
   - the child has suffered (or is exposed to a substantial risk of) physical injury or sexual abuse;
   - the child needs medical treatment for a serious condition, and the parent, guardian, or custodian is either unwilling or unable to provide or consent to the treatment;
   - a parent, guardian, or custodian consents to the child's removal from the home; or
   - the child is a runaway and consents to nonsecure custody.[5]

If the judge makes these findings and authorizes the child's removal from the home, the judge may direct a law enforcement officer to assume custody of the child and take the child to the social services office or another specified place, such as the home of a relative.[6] If the judge cannot make these findings, the child must be left in the home (or returned to the home if already taken into custody) until the case is heard in juvenile court.

Removing the child from the home before there has been a full hearing on the petition deprives the parents of custody before they have had a chance to present their side of the case. For that reason, until the full hearing the court must hold periodic hearings to determine whether grounds for keeping the child out of the home pending the hearing continue to exist.[7] Strict time limits apply to these hearings:

- If a judge entered the order for the child's placement, the first hearing must be held within seven calendar days after the child is removed from the home. If the order was entered by someone other than a judge, the hearing must be held on the earliest day possible within those seven days. This hearing may not be waived, but it may be continued for up to ten business days if the parties agree.[8]
- If the child is not returned home at the first hearing, the court must hold a second hearing within seven business days after the first hearing.[9] This and subsequent hearings may be waived if the parties agree.[10]

- For as long as the child is kept out of the home without a full hearing on the petition, the court must continue to hold these hearings at least every thirty calendar days, unless they are waived.[11]

At each of these hearings, the burden is on the department of social services to show by clear and convincing evidence that keeping the child out of the parent's custody pending a hearing on the petition is necessary.[12]

Court Representation
Child's Guardian ad Litem

Whenever a social services department files a petition alleging that a child is abused or neglected the court must appoint a special representative—a guardian ad litem—to represent the child's interests in the proceeding.[13] A guardian ad litem usually will be a volunteer working under the supervision of the judicial district's guardian ad litem program.[14] If the person appointed is not an attorney, the court also must appoint an attorney advocate to represent the child's legal interests.[15] When a petition alleges only that a child is dependent, the judge is not required to appoint a guardian ad litem and attorney advocate for the child, but it may do so.[16]

The guardian ad litem program's overall mission is to protect and promote the child's best interests. Its specific duties include

- investigating to determine the facts, the child's needs, and resources available in the family and community;
- facilitating the settlement of disputed issues;
- offering evidence and examining witnesses in court;
- exploring dispositional options; and
- conducting follow-up investigations and reporting to the court if the child's needs are not being met.[17]

The Juvenile Code authorizes guardians ad litem to obtain any information or reports, including those that are confidential, that the guardian ad litem considers relevant to the case. A guardian ad litem who is exercising this authority should present the court order that appointed him or her as the child's guardian ad litem. The guardian ad litem must protect the confidentiality of any information he or she receives.[18]

A medical or mental health provider, a school, or any other agency or professional from whom a guardian ad litem seeks information should provide the information promptly, unless

1. the person seeking the information has not presented the court order appointing him or her or otherwise established that he or she is the child's guardian ad litem, or
2. federal law or regulations prohibit disclosure of the information.[19]

Representation for Parents

In an abuse, neglect, or dependency case a child's parent, if indigent, is entitled to court-appointed counsel unless the parent waives that right.[20] In addition, the court may appoint a guardian ad litem for a parent who is incompetent.[21]

Stages in Juvenile Cases

Juvenile cases have two primary stages—adjudication and disposition. The purpose of the adjudicatory, or fact-finding, hearing is for the court to determine from the evidence whether the child is an abused, neglected, or dependent juvenile. Only after adjudicating the child to be abused, neglected, or dependent may the court continue to enter orders affecting the child's placement and care and direct orders to the child's parents.

Adjudication

At the adjudicatory hearing, the judge hears testimony, considers other evidence (such as medical records), and determines whether

1. the facts alleged in the petition are true; and
2. the facts establish that the child is an abused, neglected, or dependent juvenile within the meaning of the Juvenile Code definitions.[22]

This hearing must be held within sixty days after the petition is filed unless the court orders that it be held later.[23] The hearing is fairly formal, and the rules of evidence apply.[24] The burden is on the department of social services to prove the relevant facts by clear and convincing evidence.[25]

The judge is not required to exclude the public from the hearing but may do so after considering a list of factors set out in the Juvenile Code.[26]

The hearing must be open, however, if the child (through the guardian ad litem or attorney advocate) asks that it be open.[27] Anyone who has relevant information, including the person who made the report, may be subpoenaed to testify at the hearing.[28]

If the court does not find by clear and convincing evidence that the child is abused, neglected, or dependent, the case must be dismissed.[29] The "clear and convincing" evidence standard is stricter than the one that applies in most civil cases but less stringent than the standard that applies in criminal or delinquency cases. (Most civil cases are decided by the greater weight, or preponderance, of the evidence. Criminal or delinquency cases require proof beyond a reasonable doubt.)

Disposition

A dispositional hearing occurs only if the judge finds at the adjudication hearing that the child is abused, neglected, or dependent. This hearing should begin immediately following the adjudication and must be completed within thirty days after the adjudication hearing.[30] The hearing may be informal, and the judge may consider written reports and evidence that would not be admissible at the adjudicatory stage.[31]

The first step at this hearing is to identify the child's needs. To that end, the judge may order that the child be examined by a physician, psychiatrist, or other expert.[32] The judge may need to receive written reports or hear testimony about the child's educational, medical, psychological, or social needs. With input from all of the parties, the judge then designs an appropriate plan to meet the child's needs. In order to do this, the judge needs to receive information about the parents' ability to meet the child's needs, the parents' own needs, and available resources.[33]

The finding that a child is abused, neglected, or dependent does not automatically result in the child's removal, or continued removal, from the parents' custody. The law favors leaving the child at home when the child can be safe there.[34] The judge may postpone further hearings in order to allow the parents or others to take appropriate action or even dismiss the case if no further action is required.[35] If the child needs better care or supervision, the judge may order the department of social services to supervise the child in the child's own home, subject to conditions the judge specifies.[36] Or the judge may order that the child be placed in the custody of a parent, some other suitable person, a private agency, or the county department of social services.[37] If the disposition order provides for the child to be placed or to remain in the custody of the department of social services, the judge must make findings as to whether the department of social services has made reasonable efforts to prevent or eliminate the need for the child's placement.[38] (See "Keeping the Family Together" in Chapter 11.)

Review Hearings

The child (through the guardian ad litem or attorney advocate) or any other party may file a motion at any time asking the court to review a case. A motion for review results in a hearing at which the judge may modify a dispositional order based on a change of circumstances and the child's best interests.[39] If the dispositional order removes a child from the parent's custody, however, the court must hold review hearings according to the schedule described below.

The first review hearing must be held within ninety days after the dispositional hearing;[40] often it will be held earlier than that. If the child remains out of the home at the end of that review, a second review hearing must be held within six months after the first one. Thereafter, reviews must be held at least every six months for as long as the child remains out of the home.[41] Within a year after the child was first removed from the home, the court must hold a review hearing that is designated a "permanency planning hearing" to focus directly on whether the child will be able to return home and, if not, what the alternative permanent plan for the child should be.[42]

The county director of social services is responsible for asking the clerk of superior court to schedule these review hearings. The clerk is responsible for giving fifteen days' notice of a review hearing and its purpose to the child's parent, guardian, or custodian; the child, if he or she is twelve or older; the person providing care for the child; any agency that has custody of the child; the guardian ad litem; and anyone else the court specifies.[43]

Authority over Parents

After making proper findings at a dispositional hearing or any review hearing, the court may order that a parent who is able to do so pay a reasonable amount of support for a child who is not in the parent's custody[44] and to pay for any treatment the court orders.[45] At those same hearings the court may order a parent or a guardian, custodian, or caretaker who was served with a summons

1. to participate in medical, psychiatric, psychological, or other treatment the child needs;[46]
2. to receive psychiatric, psychological, or other treatment or counseling aimed at correcting behaviors or conditions that contributed to the child's being adjudicated or to the court's decision to remove the child from the home;[47]
3. to attend and participate in parental responsibility classes if those are available in the district where the parent, guardian, custodian, or caretaker lives;[48]
4. to provide, if able to do so, transportation for the child to keep appointments for medical, psychiatric, psychological, or other treatment the court orders;[49]
5. to take other reasonable steps to remedy the conditions that led or contributed to the child's adjudication or removal from the home.[50]

A parent or other person who has been served with a summons in the case and willfully fails to comply with the court's orders may be held in contempt.[51]

Notes

1. Chapter 7B of the North Carolina General Statutes (hereinafter G.S.). The North Carolina General Statutes can be viewed online at www.ncga.state.nc.us/gascripts/Statutes/StatutesTOC.pl. Juvenile court procedures are described in much greater detail in Kella W. Hatcher, Janet Mason, and John Rubin, *Abuse, Neglect, Dependency, and Termination of Parental Rights Proceedings in North Carolina* (Chapel Hill, N.C.: UNC School of Government, 2011) (hereinafter *Abuse, Neglect, Dependency, and Termination of Parental Rights Proceedings*). This book can be accessed, in PDF form, free of charge, at http://shopping.netsuite.com/s.nl/c.433425/it.A/id.4228/.f.

2. *See* G.S. Chapter 48 (adoptions); G.S. Chapter 122C, Article 5 (voluntary admissions and involuntary commitments of minors to mental health treatment facilities); and G.S. 50-13.1 through -13.8 (custody disputes between parents).

3. As described in Chapter 12, when the reporter seeks review of the director's decision not to file a petition, a prosecutor, after conducting the review, is authorized to direct the director to file a petition.

4. Ordinarily this type of order will be entered by a district court judge. The chief district court judge, however, may file an administrative order delegating authority to enter these orders to persons other than district court judges. G.S. 7B-502.

5. G.S. 7B-503(a).

6. G.S. 7B-504 and -505.

7. G.S. 7B-506.

8. G.S. 7B-506(a).

9. G.S. 7B-506(e).

10. G.S. 7B-506(f).

11. G.S. 7B-506(e).

12. G.S. 7B-506(b).

13. G.S. 7B-601.

14. District-level guardian ad litem programs are part of the statewide Guardian ad Litem Program, which is administered by the state Administrative Office of the Courts. *See* Article 12 of G.S. Chapter 7B.

15. G.S. 7B-601(a).

16. *Id.*

17. *Id.*

18. *Id.*

19. *See* Section 5.8C in Hatcher, Rubin, and Mason, *Abuse, Neglect, Dependency, and Termination of Parental Rights Proceedings,* cited in full in note 1.

20. G.S. 7B-602(a), (a1).

21. G.S. 7B-602(c), (d). A guardian ad litem, who may not also serve as the parent's attorney, is appointed pursuant to G.S. 1A-1, Rule 17.

22. G.S. 7B-802 and -807.

23. G.S. 7B-801(c).

24. G.S. 7B-804.

25. G.S. 7B-805.

26. G.S. 7B-801(a).

27. G.S. 7B-801(b).

28. *See* John Rubin and Aimee Wall, "Responding to Subpoenas for Health Department Records," *Health Law Bulletin* No. 82 (Sept. 2005), http://sogpubs.unc.edu/electronicversions/pdfs/hlb82.pdf; John Rubin, "Subpoenas and School Records: A School Employee's Guide." *School Law Bulletin* 30 (Spring 1999): 1–11, http://ncinfo.iog.unc.edu/pubs/electronicversions/slb/sp990111.pdf; and John Rubin and Mark Botts, "Responding to Subpoenas: A Guide for Mental Health Facilities," *Popular Government* 64 (Summer 1999): 27–38, http://ncinfo.iog.unc.edu/pubs/electronicversions/pg/botts.pdf.

29. G.S. 7B-807(a).

30. G.S. 7B-901.

31. *Id.*

32. G.S. 7B-903(a)(3).

33. G.S. 7B-901.

34. *See* G.S. 7B-900.

35. G.S. 7B-903(a)(1).

36. G.S. 7B-903(a)(2)a.

37. G.S. 7B-903(a)(2)b., c.

38. G.S. 7B-507(a).

39. G.S. 7B-1000(a).

40. G.S. 7B-906.1(a).
41. *Id.*
42. *Id.*
43. G.S. 7B-906.1(b).
44. G.S. 7B-904(d).
45. G.S. 7B-903(a)(3)a. and -904(a), (b), (c).
46. G.S. 7B-904(b).
47. G.S. 7B-904(c).
48. G.S. 7B-904(d1)(1).
49. G.S. 7B-904(d1)(2).
50. G.S. 7B-904(d1)(3).
51. G.S. 7B-904(e).

Part 5. Role of Other Agencies

Chapter 14

Schools and School Personnel

School personnel are in a unique position to recognize and respond to child abuse, neglect, and dependency. Changes in a child's behavior or appearance, as well as the child's own statements, may draw a teacher's, bus driver's, counselor's, or principal's attention to a problem others have not noticed. School personnel tend to be very aware of their reporting duties and are among the most frequent reporters.[1]

Reports to Social Services by School Personnel

The Juvenile Code does not include any special provisions relating to schools or school personnel in connection with child protection. The General Assembly, however, has emphasized the important role of school personnel by repeating the reporting mandate in Chapter 115C of the General Statutes, which contains laws relating to elementary and secondary education.

> **§ 115C-400. School personnel to report child abuse.**
> Any person who has cause to suspect child abuse or neglect has a duty to report the case of the child to the Director of Social Services of the county, as provided in Article 3 of Chapter 7B of the General Statutes [the Juvenile Code].

Although this statute does not specifically refer to cause to suspect that a child is dependent or has died as the result of maltreatment, school personnel are mandated to report in those cases as well. Indicators that a child may be dependent—that is, in need of assistance or placement because the child has no parent, guardian, or custodian[2] or because those persons are not able to provide proper care and supervision—often are the same as or similar to those that create cause to suspect neglect.

A teacher's or other school official's observations about a child may create obvious cause to suspect that the child is abused or neglected and a clear duty to make a report to social services. Frequently, however, the duty is not that clear. Following are two examples of the kinds of questions school personnel may ask in trying to understand their duty to report and social services departments' responses to reports:[3]

1. *Is a child neglected if the child comes to school inadequately clothed, dirty, or with untreated head lice?*

Although each of these observations about a child may indicate that the child is not receiving proper care and is neglected, that is not always the case. A school's initial response to concerns about a child's hygiene, inappropriate dress, or head lice is not likely to be, and ordinarily should not be, a report to social services. If the problem occurs repeatedly, is having a harmful effect on the child, and is not being addressed appropriately by the parents, however, a report to social services is required. In a particular case, whether a report is required will depend to some extent on the child's age, whether there are additional concerns about the care the child receives, and other available information about the child and the child's family. Some county social services departments may have written policies about these kinds of reports, and in some counties the social services department and the school system or individual schools develop written protocols to provide guidance about when a report should be made.

Policies of the state Division of Social Services include screening tools to guide county social services departments in determining whether a report sufficiently alleges neglect or abuse and whether a report should be accepted for assessment.[4] Some of that policy guidance is summarized below:

- Clothing. A report should be accepted and an assessment is required when the child's clothing is not sufficient to protect the child from the elements and from health hazards.
- Hygiene. Depending on the child's age and needs, a report about a child's hygiene should be accepted for assessment when a serious health hazard is present and the parent (or guardian, custodian, or caretaker) is not taking appropriate action to eliminate the problem.

- Head lice. The fact that a child has head lice, by itself, does not indicate neglect and should not be reported to social services. If a report about head lice is made, the department will want additional information—such as whether and how the parents have attempted to treat the head lice and whether the local health department or other service providers have been involved—before deciding whether to accept the report for assessment.[5]

2. *Is a child neglected if the child is repeatedly tardy or absent from school?*
Again, answering the question requires additional information.

In two cases the North Carolina Court of Appeals has held that children whose parents failed to enroll them in school were neglected juveniles.[6] In one of those cases, decided in 1987, the court found that a father's insistence on home-schooling his developmentally disabled son was neglect because it deprived the child of the socialization and special education classes that public school could provide and that were critical to the child's development and welfare.[7] In the other case, decided in 1976, parents refused to enroll their children in school because the school failed to teach about Indians and Indian heritage and culture, and the parents did not provide a sufficient alternative education.[8] "It is fundamental," the court said, "that a child who receives proper care and supervision in modern times is provided a basic education."[9]

Social services departments and the protective services laws, however, are not the appropriate avenues for responding to most school attendance issues. A child who deliberately misses school may be an "undisciplined juvenile" and subject to juvenile justice procedures designed to address the child's behavior.[10] A parent who willfully fails to comply with the law requiring parents to send their children to school can be charged with a Class 1 misdemeanor.[11] In some counties the courts, schools, and other agencies have coordinated to operate truancy court programs or truancy councils to divert truancy problems from the court system.

The responsibility for addressing attendance issues rests first with the parents and then with the school principal and other school personnel.[12] Principals have very specific duties in relation to attendance problems:[13]

- When a child has three unexcused absences, the principal is required to notify the child's parent, guardian, or custodian.[14]
- When a child has up to six unexcused absences, the principal must notify the child's parent, guardian, or custodian again, in writing and

with notice of possible criminal prosecution under the compulsory attendance law.[15]

- If a child has ten unexcused absences in a school year, the principal must take steps to determine whether the parent has made good-faith efforts to comply with the compulsory attendance law.[16]
    - If the principal determines that the parent has made good-faith efforts, the principal may file a complaint with a juvenile court counselor alleging that the student is unlawfully absent from school and therefore is an "undisciplined juvenile."[17]
    - If the principal determines that the parent has not made good-faith efforts to comply with the compulsory attendance law, the principal is required to notify both the local district attorney and the director of the county department of social services.[18] The district attorney or other prosecutor decides whether to initiate criminal charges against the parent. The social services director determines whether to treat the notification as a report of suspected neglect and undertake an assessment.[19]

Cooperative Agreements

In some counties the department of social services and the local school system (and sometimes other agencies as well) have adopted procedures for working together in responding to cases of suspected child abuse, neglect, and dependency. These procedures or protocols can clarify the roles and expectations of people in both systems. They can reflect not only what the law requires, but also local conditions, resources, and needs. Just the process of developing and reviewing local procedures can increase understanding and open lines of communication in ways that have lasting effect. The initiative for developing a local protocol for responding to abuse, neglect, and dependency may come from the school system, the department of social services, the community child protection team (see Chapter 12), or elsewhere in the community.

Guidelines developed at the state level can provide a good starting point for developing local procedures. Beginning in 1984, and most recently in 2007, the state Department of Health and Human Services and the state Department of Public Instruction have agreed on recommended procedures to "facilitate cooperation and collaboration" between local school systems and county social services departments in responding to suspected child abuse and neglect.[20] A local agency or group that is considering developing local policies should determine whether these recommended procedures have been revised.[21]

Sample Provisions for Cooperative Agreements

Beyond ensuring compliance with the legal requirements for reporting and responding to reports, there is no one best policy or set of procedures to guide local agencies. Following are examples of the kinds of provisions a local agreement might include. Some of them are adapted from the state recommended procedures described above.

1. Adoption of Policies
   - Specify the group of people responsible for developing and periodically reviewing the local policies.
   - Describe ways in which input will be sought from others who have an interest in the procedures.
   - Indicate what persons or bodies should formally approve or adopt the policies—for example, the county social services director and local school superintendent(s), or the county social services board and the local school board(s).
   - Establish a timetable and procedure for periodically reviewing the policies.
   - Describe how the policies will be published and distributed or otherwise made available.

2. Reports by School Personnel to Social Services
   - Require that all school personnel be informed of their responsibilities relating to child abuse, neglect, and dependency; the ability of the social services department to receive reports any day and any time of day or night; and how reports should be made.
   - Decide whether each local school may (or shall) designate a contact person (and a backup) to receive reports from school employees and convey them to the department of social services. If this policy is adopted, it should also make clear that
     ○ the designated person must transmit any report of suspected abuse or neglect to social services immediately;

- the report must identify the originator of the report and include information about how the department of social services can contact that person;
- if a school employee believes these procedures would create a delay that would be detrimental to the child, the employee must make a report directly to the social services department and then inform the contact person; and
- every school employee is free to contact the department of social services about a report the employee initiated and should be encouraged to cooperate with the department with respect to the report and any resulting assessment.
- Provide that school personnel should gather only enough information to validate that there is cause to suspect abuse, neglect, or dependency, since it is not the responsibility of school officials or employees to conduct investigations.
- Describe circumstances, if any, under which a school official, at the request of the department of social services, will photograph a child or take other specified steps to aid the department in conducting an assessment; also describe any actions school officials should not be asked or expected to take.

3. Social Services Response
   - Indicate whether the department of social services will designate a contact person (and a backup) to receive inquiries from and convey information to school officials about reported cases of abuse, neglect, or dependency.
   - State how and to whom the department will provide the written notices regarding whether a report is accepted for assessment and the outcome of an assessment. Also specify when, if ever, the right to receive a written notification is or may be waived or when the notification may be given orally.
   - Describe circumstances in which it is appropriate for a social worker to interview the child (or other children in the same family) at school.
   - Specify procedures for a social worker to notify the principal or the school contact person to arrange a mutually convenient time that is least disruptive to the child's schedule and the school generally.

- Specify criteria and procedures for determining whether and how a parent, guardian, or custodian will be notified about the interview or invited to be present for it.
- Establish criteria for determining which if any school or law enforcement personnel should be present when a social worker interviews a child at school, making clear that the social worker always has authority to insist on seeing the child alone.[22]

4. Cooperation between Schools and Social Services
   - Describe ways in which school personnel will cooperate with the social worker in the assessment, such as
     - giving the social worker any information that could help establish whether abuse or neglect has occurred or the child is dependent;
     - allowing the social worker to interview the child alone;
     - allowing the social worker to photograph any evidence, such as marks or bruises;
     - allowing the social worker to remove the child from the school if the social worker determines that the child is at immediate risk. (This will require a court order unless the statutory conditions for temporary custody without a court order exist. See "Immediate Removal of Child" in Chapter 11.)
   - Acknowledge that, within any federal law constraints, social services personnel and school personnel may share with each other confidential information relating to the child when the information will be used
     - for the protection of the child,
     - for the protection of others, or
     - to improve the child's educational opportunities.[23]
   (See "When Disclosure Is Allowed" in Chapter 11.)

5. Follow-up
   - Describe procedures for the notifications that the social services department provides to the school contact person to be shared promptly with the individual who initiated the report.
   - Describe ways in which the two agencies will collaborate in planning consistent services for the child and the child's family.

- Establish policies and procedures for enabling a child to remain in the same school, if at all possible, when the child is placed in foster care or other out-of-home placement.

6. General
   - Provide for joint training and learning opportunities for school personnel and social services personnel, including opportunities for each to become better informed about the role of the other.
   - Describe how the department of social services and the school system will use their participation in the community child protection team to improve their responses to child abuse, neglect, and dependency. (See "Community Child Protection Teams" in Chapter 12.)

Reporting in Relation to License Suspension and Revocation

Mistreatment of children at school by teachers or other school personnel is not "abuse" or "neglect" within the Juvenile Code definitions because those people are not the child's caretakers or custodians.[24] (See Chapters 4 and 5.) Although social services departments do not have a role in investigating and responding to the mistreatment of children at school, school administrators certainly do.

A rule of the State Board of Education requires local school administrators[25] to report to the state superintendent of public instruction any time they know, or have reason to believe, that a certified school employee has engaged in behavior that

1. would justify revoking the employee's certificate, and
2. involves physical or sexual abuse of a child.[26]

"Physical abuse" for purposes of this requirement means the infliction of non-accidental physical injury by means that are not in self-defense.[27] Corporal punishment, by contrast, is the "intentional infliction of physical pain" for purposes of discipline and should never result in injury.[28] The term "sexual abuse" means the commission of a sexual act on a student or causing a student to commit a sexual act. Neither the student's age nor whether the student consented is relevant.[29] An administrator's failure to make a required report is, in itself, a ground for suspending or revoking the administrator's certificate.[30] Local school boards may have policies that impose similar internal reporting requirements on other school personnel.

Reporting Certain Criminal Acts

Another reporting requirement applies to some instances of abuse or neglect of a child, as well as a number of other criminal or delinquent acts, that occur at school. A school principal is required to report immediately to the appropriate local law enforcement agency any time the principal has personal knowledge or actual notice from school personnel that one of the following acts has occurred on school property:

- assault resulting in serious personal injury,
- sexual assault,
- sexual offense,
- rape,
- kidnapping,
- indecent liberties with a minor,
- assault involving the use of a weapon,
- unlawful possession of a firearm,
- unlawful possession of a weapon, or
- unlawful possession of a controlled substance.[31]

This reporting requirement applies regardless of the age or status of the offender or the victim (if the offense involves a victim). The act could be committed either by or against a student, a teacher or other employee, a parent, a trespasser, or anyone else. The report to law enforcement is required only if the act occurs on school property, which includes any public school building, bus, campus, grounds, recreational area, or athletic field in the principal's charge.[32]

When a principal makes a required report to law enforcement, the principal (or his or her designee) also must notify the superintendent (or his or her designee) of the report. The notification may be given in writing or by electronic mail. It should be made the same day the incident occurred, if possible, but must be made no later than the end of the following workday. The superintendent then must provide the information to the local school board.[33] Every local board of education is required to have a policy on notifying the parent or legal guardian of any student who is alleged to be the victim of any of the acts the principal is required to report to law enforcement and the superintendent.[34]

Notes

1. Conditions that require reporting by school personnel are discussed in Chapter 5.

2. The terms "parent," "guardian," and "custodian" are discussed in Chapter 4.

3. See Chapter 11 for a related discussion of screening—the process by which social services departments decide whether to accept reports for assessment.

4. N.C. Department of Health & Human Services, Division of Social Services, "Instructions for Completion of Structured Intake Report/CPS Intake Report Tool, DSS-1402," *in* Section 1407.V., Chapter VIII, of the Division of Social Services' online *Family Support and Child Welfare Manual* (hereinafter *State Manual*), http://info.dhhs.state.nc.us/olm/manuals/dss/csm-60/man/CS1407-04.htm#TopOfPage.

5. "Instructions for Completion of Structured Intake Report/CPS Intake Report Tool, DSS-1402," *in* Section 1407.V., Chapter VIII, *State Manual*, cited in full in note 4.

6. *In re* Devone, 86 N.C. App. 57, 356 S.E.2d 389 (1987); *In re* McMillan, 30 N.C. App. 235, 226 S.E.2d 693 (1976).

7. *Devone*, 86 N.C. App. at 60–61, 356 S.E.2d at 391.

8. *McMillan*, 30 N.C. App. at 236, 226 S.E.2d at 694.

9. *Id.* at 238, 226 S.E.2d at 695.

10. These procedures are set out in Subchapter II of the Juvenile Code, North Carolina General Statutes (hereinafter G.S.) §§ 7B-1500 through -2827. The North Carolina General Statutes can be viewed online at www.ncga.state.nc.us/gascripts/Statutes/StatutesTOC.pl.

11. G.S. 115C-380. The compulsory attendance laws, G.S. 115C-378 through -383, require "[e]very parent, guardian or custodian in this State having charge or control of a child between the ages of seven and 16 years [to] cause the child to attend school continuously for a period equal to the time which the public school to which the child is assigned shall be in session." G.S. 115C-378(a). The likelihood that violations of the compulsory attendance law will be prosecuted varies substantially among judicial and prosecutorial districts.

12. *See* G.S. 115C-379.

13. *See* G.S. 115C-378.

14. G.S. 115C-378(e).

15. *Id.*

16. G.S. 115C-378(f).

17. *Id.* "Undisciplined juvenile" is defined in G.S. 7B-1501(27).

18. G.S. 115C-378(f).

19. *Id.*

20. The most recent untitled agreement, which became effective January 22, 2007, was signed by Sherry Bradsher, Director, Division of Social Services, and Dr. June

Atkinson, State Superintendent, Department of Public Instruction. The agreement is available at www.ncdhhs.gov/dss/dcdl/famsupchildwelfare/fscw-08-2007a.pdf.

21. Additional guidance for reporting by school personnel can be found in N.C. Department of Health & Human Services, School Health Unit, North Carolina Public Health, North Carolina Healthy Schools, *North Carolina School Health Program Manual*, 5th ed. (2010), B1-1 to B1-15, www.ncdhhs.gov/dph/wch/doc/lhd/nc_school_health_program_manual_2010.pdf.

22. Refusing to allow the social services director (which includes the director's representative) to see a child alone constitutes obstructing or interfering with a protective services assessment. G.S. 7B-303(b).

23. G.S. 7B-3100(a). The sharing of school information must be in accordance with the Family Educational Rights and Privacy Act (FERPA), 20 U.S.C. § 1232g.

24. *See* G.S. 7B-101(3) and (8).

25. For purposes of the rule, school administrators include superintendents, assistant superintendents, associate superintendents, personnel administrators, and principals. N.C. Admin. Code (hereinafter N.C.A.C.) tit. 16, subch. 6C, § .0312(b) (Dec. 2004).

26. *Id.*

27. *Id.*

28. G.S. 115C-390.1(b)(2). See also G.S. 115C-390.4 and -391.1, which address the permissible use in schools of corporal punishment and seclusion and restraint, respectively.

29. N.C.A.C. tit. 16, subch. 6C, § .0312(b).

30. N.C.A.C. tit. 16, subch. 6C, § .0312(a)(9).

31. G.S. 115C-288(g). The statute prohibits the State Board of Education from requiring principals to report acts to law enforcement beyond those the law requires them to report. *Id.*

32. *Id.*

33. G.S. 115C-288(g).

34. G.S. 115C-47(56).

Chapter 15

Health and Mental Health Professionals and Facilities

Reporting

Child abuse and neglect often are identified for the first time when a child is taken to an emergency room or other medical facility or provider for treatment. As discussed in Chapter 2, the very first child abuse reporting laws were designed largely to override doctor–patient confidentiality so that doctors could disclose information about children they saw who were abused without violating confidentiality requirements. Although reporting laws have expanded to cover many other professionals—and in North Carolina, to cover everyone—health care professionals continue to be a key source of reports of child abuse, neglect, and dependency. (For definitions of the conditions that require reporting by medical personnel, see Chapter 5, "The Conditions Defined: Neglect, Abuse, Dependency, and Maltreatment.")

In addition to the duty to report suspected child abuse, neglect, or dependency to a department of social services, physicians and hospitals have long had a duty to make reports directly to law enforcement in some instances. This duty, which may apply when patients are adults as well as when they are children, exists when a physician or hospital learns of

- an injury that appears to be caused by or related to the discharge of a firearm, poisoning, or use of a knife or sharp instrument if it appears that a criminal act occurred; or
- a grave bodily injury or grave illness that appears to be the result of an act of criminal violence.[1]

In 2008, the North Carolina General Assembly expanded medical personnel's duty to report to law enforcement to include

> cases involving recurrent illness or serious physical injury to any child under the age of 18 years where the illness or injury appears, in the physician's professional judgment, to be the result of nonaccidental trauma.[2]

The report is required without regard to who may have caused the child's injury or illness. In some cases reports will be required both to law enforcement, pursuant to this duty, and to the county department of social services because there is cause to suspect that a child victim is abused, neglected, or dependent. Anyone who makes a good-faith report to law enforcement or social services, or to both, has immunity from civil or criminal liability.[3] Although immunity does not guarantee that a civil or criminal action will not be brought against someone who makes a report, unless the person bringing such an action alleges and can prove that the report was made in bad faith—that is, maliciously—the action should be quickly dismissed.

Professional Ethics and Reporting Responsibilities

Health care professionals sometimes confront very difficult issues when trying to honor both their statutory duty to report suspected child abuse, neglect, and dependency and their professional ethic of confidentiality.[4] *Confidentiality* refers to the ethical mandate to protect patient and client privacy, and it is considered a cornerstone of the professional, treatment, or therapeutic relationship. Conflicts may occur, for example, when a psychotherapist becomes aware that a young client or patient has been victimized or that an adult client or patient may have harmed a child.

The statutory requirement to report supersedes confidentiality.[5] At the same time, the ethical codes of psychologists, physicians, counselors, social workers, and others require that these professionals not exceed the reporting that is required by law. Health care professionals, therefore, are sensitive to the fine points of the meaning of key terms such as *caretaker, abuse, neglect,* and *serious physical injury.* (These terms are discussed in Chapters 4 and 5.) In addition to making reports only when the law requires reporting, professionals must consider the scope of information they can properly disclose when making a report. It may be helpful to remember that the duty to report includes a duty to include in the report, to the extent the person making the report knows,

1. the nature and extent of any injury or condition resulting from abuse, neglect, or dependency; and
2. any other information the person making the report believes might be helpful in determining the need for protective services or court intervention.[6]

After a report is made—and regardless of who made the report—a health care professional may be required to disclose confidential information. In conducting an assessment or providing protective services, the social services director (or the director's representative) is authorized to make a written demand on any agency or individual for any information or reports that are relevant to the assessment or to the provision of protective services.[7] Unless the information is protected by the attorney–client privilege or its disclosure is prohibited by federal law, the agency or individual is required to give the director access to and copies of the information.[8] If a juvenile court action is filed and the court appoints a guardian ad litem to represent the child's interests, that individual has similar authority to acquire confidential information relevant to the case.[9] And, of course, the court can order the disclosure of confidential information.

A health or mental health professional who exceeds his or her legal reporting responsibilities, thereby violating a patient's or client's confidentiality without statutory authority to do so, risks being sanctioned for an ethics violation within his or her profession. In other words, a fine line separates required and prohibited reporting for professionals with obligations of confidentiality.

The statutes that mandate reporting, however, do not operate alone in setting parameters on when a health or mental health professional can or should disclose confidential information without a client's or patient's consent. Neither the ethical duty to maintain confidentiality nor the statutory doctor–patient privilege is absolute. So, even when it is clear that there is no duty to report to social services—for example, because the person who harmed a child is not a parent, guardian, custodian, or caretaker—health care professionals should consider whether they have legal authority or an ethical or moral duty to take other action to protect clients, patients, or others from serious and foreseeable harm.

Federal law strictly controls the disclosure of protected health information. It allows a disclosure when a provider in good faith believes it is "necessary to prevent or lessen a serious and imminent threat to the health or safety of a person or the public," but the disclosure may be made only to someone who is "reasonably able to prevent or lessen the threat."[10]

North Carolina statutes and court opinions provide some guidance. A mental health confidentiality statute, for example, lists numerous instances in which a mental health professional may disclose confidential information, including "when in his opinion there is an imminent danger to the health or safety of the client or another individual or there is a likelihood of the commission of a felony or violent misdemeanor."[11] The North Carolina Court of Appeals has held that the doctor–patient privilege does not apply in involuntary commitment proceedings.[12] But neither state statutes nor case law has fully explored the scope of potential exceptions to the duty to protect a client's or patient's confidentiality.

In a frequently cited California case, *Tarasoff v. Regents of University of California*,[13] the court held that a psychiatrist who knows or should know that a patient presents a danger to a third person has a duty to warn the intended victim. In a much more recent North Carolina case, a woman's estate sued a psychiatrist for alleged negligence in failing to warn a wife of her husband's violent propensities and failing to have the husband involuntarily committed. Affirming the trial court's dismissal of the action, the North Carolina Court of Appeals held that "unlike the holding in *Tarasoff*, North Carolina does not recognize a psychiatrist's *duty to warn* third persons."[14] Despite the fact that this was a case of first impression in North Carolina, the court did not analyze the holdings of courts in other states that have considered the issue or provide any rationale for its conclusion that no such duty exists in this state.

Health care professionals must be familiar with their own codes of professional ethics. They should contact the ethics bodies of their professional associations or their licensing boards for guidance when conflicts between a duty or desire to report or provide information and the obligation to respect confidentiality are difficult to resolve. In keeping with the doctrine of informed consent for the provision of professional services, these professionals also should make clients and patients aware of the exceptions to confidentiality as part of the process of contracting for evaluation and treatment services. Finally, health care professionals who have been trained in other states need to become familiar with the North Carolina statutes. Reporting laws, although universal, differ dramatically from state to state in their specific provisions and definitions.

"Baby Doe": Disabled Infants with Life-Threatening Conditions

The federal Child Abuse Amendments of 1984 required states, as a condition of receiving certain federal child welfare funds, to include in their definitions of "neglected juvenile" a specific category of disabled infants from whom treatment is being withheld.[15] In 1985, the North Carolina Social Services Commission adopted a rule that defined "neglected juvenile" to include a specific reference to those disabled infants,[16] but in 2006 the rule was rewritten and the definition of "neglected juvenile" was deleted altogether. The Juvenile Code defines "neglected juvenile" to include a child who is "not provided necessary medical care" but includes no specific reference to these disabled infants.[17]

In 2008, the state Division of Social Services added to its child welfare policy manual provisions that address this category of infant in some detail.[18] The manual provision, mirroring the wording in federal law, states that a disabled infant (under one year of age) with a life-threatening condition is "neglected" if

1. the infant is being denied appropriate nutrition, hydration, or medication; or
2. the infant is not receiving medically indicated treatment that, in the treating physician's reasonable medical judgment, is most likely to be effective in ameliorating or correcting the life-threatening condition, unless it is also the physician's reasonable medical judgment
   - that the infant is chronically ill and irreversibly comatose; or
   - that medical treatment would merely prolong dying, would not ameliorate or correct all of the life-threatening conditions, or would otherwise be futile in terms of the infant's survival; or
   - that the provision of medical treatment would be virtually futile in terms of the infant's survival, and under the circumstances the treatment would be inhumane.[19]

The state policy manual also requires every county social services director to

- make contact with every hospital or health care facility in the county that treats infants;
- provide each hospital or facility with information about the mandatory reporting law and procedures, including specific contact information, for making reports both during and after working hours; and
- obtain the name and telephone number of the person in the hospital or facility who will act as a liaison with the county social services department and update this information at least yearly.[20]

Substance-Exposed Infants

If a child tests positive at birth for illegal drug exposure, is the child abused (or neglected or dependent)? Answering that question requires additional information. However, as discussed below, indications of prenatal drug exposure are sufficient to create "cause to suspect" abuse, neglect, or dependency and to require a report to the county department of social services.

States' responses to children who show evidence at birth of exposure to alcohol or drugs vary. Some states have enacted specific reporting requirements relating to these children, and others have amended their reporting laws to include these children's conditions in the abuse and neglect definitions that determine what must be reported.[21] One state supreme court, interpreting a state statute that did not refer specifically to drug-exposed infants, held that a newborn who tests positive for an illegal drug at birth due to the mother's drug abuse "is *per se* an abused child."[22]

In North Carolina, neither the Juvenile Code nor any appellate court decision says that a child's testing positive for drugs at birth, without more, is sufficient to render the child an abused, neglected, or dependent juvenile. However, the federal Child Abuse Prevention and Treatment Act includes a child welfare funding condition that requires states' social services departments to accept reports about substance-exposed infants, conduct assessments, and develop protection plans for these children.[23] The federal law requires a state that accepts funds under Title IV-E of the Social Security Act, as North Carolina does, to provide assurance that the state either has and is enforcing a law, or is operating a program, that includes the following:

(ii) policies and procedures (including appropriate referrals to child protection service systems and for other appropriate services) to address the needs of infants born and identified as being affected by illegal substance abuse or withdrawal symptoms resulting from prenatal drug exposure, or a Fetal Alcohol Spectrum Disorder, including a requirement that health care providers involved in the delivery or care of such infants notify the child protective services system of the occurrence of such condition in such infants,

. . .

(iii) the development of a plan of safe care for the infant born and identified as being affected by illegal substance abuse or withdrawal symptoms, or a Fetal Alcohol Spectrum Disorder. [24]

In addition, the federal Individuals with Disabilities Education Act requires that states mandate the referral for early intervention services of any child under age three who is (1) involved in a substantiated case of abuse or neglect or (2) identified as being affected by illegal substance abuse or having withdrawal symptoms as a result of prenatal drug exposure.[25]

Policy of the North Carolina Division of Social Services states that "prenatal drug exposure does not constitute neglect per se" but that the county social services department "has a responsibility to assure that the living environment will not be injurious to the newborn."[26] County social services departments expect hospitals to make reports when there are indications that a newborn has been exposed to alcohol or drugs. They accept these reports and conduct assessments in response to them. However, the department's assessment must extend beyond the question of whether the infant tested positive at birth for alcohol or drugs. A report will be substantiated only if the social services department also finds

1. that the child is not receiving or will not receive proper care from the child's parent, guardian, custodian, or caretaker; or
2. that the parent is not able to provide proper care for the child and does not have a suitable alternative arrangement.[27]

In other words, the child's condition is assessed in terms of the care the child receives or is likely to receive after birth, not on the basis of the mother's conduct before the child was born.

Emergency Custody in Abuse Cases
Procedures

In an emergency, either a law enforcement officer or a social worker with a county department of social services may take a child into temporary physical custody without a court order. An emergency exists when there is reasonable cause to believe

1. that the child is abused, neglected, or dependent; and
2. that the child would be injured or could not be taken into custody if the officer or social worker first took time to obtain a court order.[28]

Social services then must further assess the case and determine whether to file a petition and seek a court order allowing social services to retain custody of the child pending a court hearing.

When someone brings a child to a medical facility for diagnosis or treatment and a physician or other person at the facility has cause to suspect that the child has been abused, that person obviously must make a report to the department of social services. In an emergency, as defined above, that person probably would seek the assistance of a law enforcement officer or social services worker who could take the child into custody immediately. Occasionally, however, a parent may attempt to take the child from the medical facility before a social worker or law enforcement officer can arrive.

The Juvenile Code provides a special procedure through which a physician or an administrator of a medical facility may seek authority from a district court judge to keep physical custody of a child and provide necessary treatment if there is cause to suspect that the child has been abused.[29] The four steps in this process are as follows:

1. Certify need to retain custody. A physician who examines the child certifies in writing that the child is suspected of being abused and should remain at the facility for medical treatment or that, based on the medical evaluation, it is unsafe for the child to return to the parent, guardian, custodian, or caretaker.
2. Obtain judicial authority. The physician or administrator contacts, most likely by telephone, the chief district court judge (or someone the judge has designated to act in his or her place) and asks for authorization to retain physical custody of the child in the facility.[30] The date and time that the physician or administrator receives judicial

authorization to retain custody must be noted on the physician's written certification.

3. Notify director of social services. If authorization to retain custody is granted, the physician or administrator (or someone that person designates) immediately notifies the director of the department of social services in the county in which the facility is located—even if the child's residence is in a different county. The director will treat the notification as a report of suspected abuse and begin an assessment.

4. Distribute copies of certification. A copy of the certification is given to the child's parent, guardian, custodian, or caretaker. Copies also are placed in the child's medical and court records.

These procedures are likely to work well only if judges, medical professionals, and social services professionals in the community are familiar with them before an emergency arises. Medical professionals and facilities need to know

- who the chief district court judge is and who, if anyone, he or she has designated to authorize custody in these cases;
- how to contact the chief district court judge or any designee(s); and
- whether forms to facilitate the required documentation are available locally—from the court, medical facilities, or the social services department—or should be developed.

It is important to remember that these procedures apply only in cases of suspected abuse, not in cases in which a child's neglect or dependency is the cause for the medical professional's concern. Even in abuse cases the procedure is not mandatory. The physician or administrator may make the required report to social services about the suspected abuse and rely on a law enforcement officer or social worker to assume temporary custody of the child if that is called for.

Time Limits and Juvenile Court Action

Authorization pursuant to this procedure allows the child to be kept in the medical facility without the parents' consent or a court order for up to twelve hours. The department of social services, however, may file a juvenile court petition and obtain a nonsecure custody order authorizing continued custody, as long as it is able to do so within the twelve-hour period. (This period is twenty-four hours if any part of the twelve-hour period falls on a weekend or holiday.) The social services department must file a petition within that time period if its preliminary assessment shows that

1. in the certifying physician's opinion, the child needs medical treatment to cure or alleviate physical distress or to prevent the child from suffering serious physical injury; and
2. in the physician's opinion, the child should remain in the custody of the facility for at least twelve hours; and
3. the parent, guardian, custodian, or caretaker either cannot be reached or will not consent to the child's treatment in the facility.

The petition will be heard in juvenile court like any other juvenile petition alleging abuse. Only the social services director and the certifying physician, together, can voluntarily dismiss the petition.

If the facts do not meet the criteria described above that require the filing of a petition, the social services director determines after an assessment—as he or she would in any other case—whether a petition should be filed. If the social services director decides not to file a petition, the physician or administrator may ask the prosecutor to review the director's decision, as in other reports of abuse, neglect, or dependency. (See "Formal Review of Case Decisions" in Chapter 12.)

Finally, if the court determines that medical treatment the physician or facility provided to the child was necessary and appropriate, the court may charge the cost of the treatment to the child's parents, guardian, custodian, or caretaker. If the parents are not able to pay, however, the court may charge the cost of the treatment to the county of the child's residence.

Treating Child without Parent's Consent

The judicial authority for a physician or medical facility to retain custody of a child in an emergency, described above, includes authorization to provide necessary treatment for the child. Although a medical professional generally cannot legally provide treatment for a child without the consent of the child's parent (or guardian or a person standing in loco parentis to the child) or a court order, a physician may treat a child without either in the following circumstances:

1. a parent or other person who could provide consent cannot be located or contacted with reasonable diligence during the time within which the child needs to receive the treatment; or
2. the child's identity is not known, or the necessity for immediate treatment is apparent and the delay caused by any effort to obtain consent would endanger the child's life; or
3. the delay caused by an attempt to contact a parent or other person who could give consent would seriously worsen the child's physical condition.[31]

If the treatment the child needs involves a surgical procedure, the surgeon must obtain a second physician's agreement that the surgery is necessary.[32] However, in a rural area or community where the surgeon is not able to contact another physician, this requirement does not apply.[33]

When a minor has the capacity to give informed consent, the minor's consent is sufficient and parental consent is not required when the minor seeks medical care for

- the prevention, diagnosis, or treatment of certain communicable diseases;
- pregnancy (but not abortion or sterilization);
- abuse of alcohol or controlled substances; or
- emotional disturbance.[34]

Judicial Authority for Emergency Medical Treatment When Parent Objects

The preceding section described a physician's authority to treat a child when a parent is not available to consent or the law does not require parental consent. If a parent is available but objects to the child's receiving treatment, a physician still may provide treatment if another physician concurs that the medical procedure is necessary to prevent immediate harm to the child.[35] If a parent refuses to consent and the physician cannot contact another physician for a concurring opinion, the procedures described below can be used to seek a district court judge's authorization to provide the treatment.[36]

1. The physician signs a statement (or, in an acute emergency, makes an oral statement to a district court judge) setting out
   - the nature of the emergency and the needed treatment, and
   - the parent's refusal to consent to the treatment, and
   - the impossibility of contacting a second physician for a concurring opinion on the need for treatment in time to prevent immediate harm to the child.[37]
2. A judge examines the physician's written statement (or considers the physician's oral statement) and finds
   - that it complies with the statute, and
   - that the proposed treatment is necessary to prevent immediate harm to the child.
3. The judge issues written authorization for the proposed treatment or, in an acute emergency, authorizes treatment in person or by telephone.
4. If either the physician's statement or the judge's authorization is oral, it is reduced to writing as soon as possible. The judge's written authorization for treatment should be issued in duplicate as follows:
   - one copy for the treating physician, and
   - one copy to be attached to the physician's written statement and filed as a juvenile proceeding in the office of the clerk of superior court.
5. After a judge authorizes treatment in this manner, and after proper notice, the judge conducts a hearing on the question of payment for the treatment, with two possible results:
   - the judge may order the parent or other responsible parties to pay for the treatment; or
   - if the judge finds that the parent is not able to pay, the judge may order that the costs of the treatment be charged to the county.

Depriving a child of necessary medical care is a form of neglect, and a physician or other person who believes that a parent is refusing to consent to necessary medical treatment for a child must make a report to the county department of social services.

Child Medical Evaluation Program/
Child Family Evaluation Program

A thorough assessment of suspected child abuse or neglect often requires the assistance of a medical or mental health professional.[38] The Child Medical Evaluation Program/Child Family Evaluation Program (CMEP/CFEP) coordinates medical and mental health professionals who are available across the state to assist county social services departments in assessing whether a child has been abused or neglected. A child medical evaluation assesses the condition of a child who may have been abused or neglected. A child/family evaluation, usually conducted by a psychologist, provides a more extensive assessment of the family unit.[39] The CMEP/CFEP operates through a contractual arrangement between the North Carolina Division of Social Services and the Department of Pediatrics at the University of North Carolina at Chapel Hill School of Medicine.

The program provides medical and psychological assessments through a roster of participating professionals with specific training relating to child abuse and neglect. While an assessment may identify a child's and his or her family's treatment needs, the program does not include the provision of ongoing medical or psychological services.[40]

The program has contributed to understanding and coordination between social services and medical professionals, accessible and appropriate evaluations of children who may be abused or neglected, better testimony and evidence in cases that go to court, and increased skills and awareness among large numbers of professionals who are involved in these cases.

The program's staff at the University of North Carolina at Chapel Hill provide training for participating medical and mental health providers and also participate frequently in training for social workers, law enforcement officers, and judges.

Notes

1. North Carolina General Statutes (hereinafter G.S.) § 90-21.20(b). The North Carolina General Statutes can be viewed online at www.ncga.state.nc.us/gascripts/Statutes/StatutesTOC.pl.

2. G.S. 90-21.20(c1).

3. G.S. 7B-309 and 90-21.20(d).

4. This section is based in part on comments submitted to the author by William V. Burlingame, Ph.D., January 3, 2001, for a previous edition of this book. Dr. Burlingame and others discussed the intersection of legal and ethical issues relating to reporting in Erica Wise, Ph.D., "Child Abuse/Neglect Reporting: Issues and Controversies," *National Register of Health Service Providers in Psychology* (Fall 2010), www.nationalregister.org/trr_fall10_wise.html.

5. See G.S. 7B-310, providing that privileges are not grounds for failing to report suspected child abuse, neglect, or dependency or for excluding evidence in a court proceeding.

6. G.S. 7B-301.

7. G.S. 7B-302(e).

8. *Id.*

9. G.S. 7B-601(c).

10. 45 C.F.R. § 164.512(j) (Oct. 1, 2011), which is part of the privacy regulations promulgated under the authority of the Administrative Simplification provisions of the Health Insurance Portability and Accountability Act of 1996 (HIPAA), 42 U.S.C. §§ 1320d–1320d-9 (2010).

11. G.S. 122C-55(d). The statute gives this authority to a "responsible professional," which G.S. 122C-3(32) defines as "an individual within a facility who is designated by the facility director to be responsible for the care, treatment, habilitation, or rehabilitation of a specific client and who is eligible to provide care, treatment, habilitation, or rehabilitation relative to the client's disability." While this might seem to restrict the scope of the disclosure authorization to those who work in certain settings, it must be read along with the definition of "facility," which "means any person at one location whose primary purpose is to provide services for the care, treatment, habilitation, or rehabilitation of the mentally ill, the developmentally disabled, or substance abusers." G.S. 122C-3(14).

12. *In re* Farrow, 41 N.C. App. 680, 683, 255 S.E.2d 777, 779–80 (1979).

13. 17 Cal. 3d 425, 131 Cal. Rptr. 14, 551 P.2d 334 (1976).

14. Gregory v. Kilbride, 150 N.C. App. 601, 610, 565 S.E.2d 685, 692 (2002), *review denied*, 357 N.C. 164, 580 S.E.2d 365 (2003).

15. *See* 42 U.S.C. 5106g(5); 45 C.F.R. § 1340.15(b).

16. N.C. Admin. Code (hereinafter N.C.A.C.) tit. 10A, subch. 70A, § .0104 (Nov. 1985).

17. *See* G.S. 7B-101(15).

18. *See* N.C. Department of Health & Human Services, Division of Social Services, "Medical Neglect of Disabled Infants with Life Threatening Conditions," *in* Section 1438, Chapter VIII, of the Division of Social Services' online *Family Support and Child Welfare Manual* (hereinafter *State Manual*), http://info.dhhs.state.nc.us/olm/manuals/dss/csm-60/man/CS1438.htm#TopOfPage. The entire manual and manuals for other social services programs can be accessed from http://info.dhhs.state.nc.us/olm/manuals/manuals.aspx?dc=dss.

19. *Id.* Comparable language is in federal regulations at 45 C.F.R. § 1340.15, www.gpo.gov/fdsys/pkg/CFR-2011-title45-vol4/pdf/CFR-2011-title45-vol4-sec1340-15.pdf. *See also* Appendix to Part 1340—Interpretative Guidelines Regarding 45 CFR 1340.15—Services

and Treatment for Disabled Infants, www.gpo.gov/fdsys/pkg/CFR-2011-title45-vol4/pdf/
CFR-2011-title45-vol4-part1340-app-id628.pdf.

20. *See* "Medical Neglect of Disabled Infants with Life Threatening Conditions," *in* Section 1438, Chapter VIII, *State Manual*, cited in full in note 18, http://
info.dhhs.state.nc.us/olm/manuals/dss/csm-60/man/CS1438.htm#TopOfPage.

21. *See* U.S. Department of Health & Human Services, Administration for Children
& Families, Child Welfare Information Gateway, "Parental Drug Use as Child Abuse:
Summary of State Laws," May 2009, www.childwelfare.gov/systemwide/laws_policies/
statutes/drugexposed.cfm.

22. *In re* Baby Boy Blackshear, 90 Ohio St. 3d 197, 200, 736 N.E.2d 462, 465 (2000)
[interpreting a statute that defined "abused child" to include one who "[b]ecause of
the acts of his parents, . . . suffers physical or mental injury that harms or threatens to
harm the child's health or welfare," *id.* at 199, 736 N.E.2d at 464 (internal quotation
marks, citations omitted)].

23. U.S. Department of Health & Human Services, Administration for Children &
Families, The Child Abuse Prevention and Treatment Act, *Including Adoption Opportunities & The Abandoned Infants Assistance Act, As Amended by* P.L. 111-320, The
CAPTA Reauthorization Act of 2010, www.acf.hhs.gov/programs/cb/laws_policies/
cblaws/capta/capta2010.pdf.

24. 42 U.S.C. §§ 5106a(b)(2)(B)(ii), (iii).

25. 20 U.S.C. § 1437(a)(6).

26. *See* "The Impact of Drug and Alcohol Abuse," *in* Section 1440.XI, Chapter VIII,
State Manual, cited in full in note 18, http://info.dhhs.state.nc.us/olm/manuals/dss/
csm-60/man/CS1440-10.htm#P213_31521.

27. A substantiation, if one is made, most likely would be based on the child's status
as a neglected child if the child is not receiving proper care or supervision, or as a
dependent child if the parent is not able to provide adequate care. *See* G.S. 7B-101(9)
and (15).

28. G.S. 7B-500. Custody without a court order can continue for only twelve hours
or, if part of that time occurs on a weekend or holiday, twenty-four hours. Except in an
emergency, a child may be taken into custody only with a court order. G.S. 7B-501(b).

29. G.S. 7B-308. The evolution of this law is interesting. In the early 1970s, former
G.S. 110-118(d) gave a physician authority on his or her own to retain temporary
physical custody of the child in this circumstance. It put the burden on the parents
to seek a court hearing if they objected. A 1975 amendment added a requirement
that the physician who retained custody of a child ask social services to file a petition
and seek a court order for temporary custody. In 1977, another amendment added
authority for the medical facility to render necessary medical treatment to the child.
The requirement that the physician get authorization from a district court judge to
retain custody of the child appeared first in the 1979 rewrite of the Juvenile Code, and
it has been in the law since then. *See* 1979 Sess. Laws ch. 815, sec. 1.

30. The statute authorizes the chief district court judge to designate someone to
act in his or her place in regard to this procedure and does not restrict whom the chief
judge may designate. It seems clear from the wording of the statute (G.S. 7B-308) that
this authority must be sought on a case-by-case basis and that a chief district court

judge should not attempt to use an administrative order or other means to give a facility or physician blanket authority to assume custody in cases of suspected abuse.

31. G.S. 90-21.1.

32. G.S. 90-21.3.

33. *Id.*

34. G.S. 90-21.5. A minor can obtain an abortion without the consent of a parent, guardian, or custodian only in a medical emergency or after obtaining a court order waiving the requirement for parental consent. G.S. 90-21.6 to 90-21.10.

35. G.S. 90-21.1

36. G.S. 7B-3600.

37. See G.S. 90-21.1, described above, which addresses when a physician may treat a minor without the consent of the parent.

38. *See In re* Browning, 124 N.C. App. 190, 194, 476 S.E.2d 465, 467 (1996) (holding that a parent's objection to his children being evaluated, although based in part on his religious beliefs, was not a lawful excuse for interfering with a social services investigation).

39. The Child/Family Evaluation Program replaced the Child Mental Health Evaluation Program (CMHEP), which also was known as the Child Forensic Evaluation Program.

40. Extensive information about the program is available on its website, University of North Carolina at Chapel Hill, School of Medicine, *Child Medical Evaluation Program*, www.med.unc.edu/cmep. The Child/Family Evaluation Program is described at www.med.unc.edu/cmep/services/cfep-training. *See also* Section 1422, Chapter VIII, *State Manual*, cited in full in note 18, http://info.dhhs.state.nc.us/olm/manuals/dss/csm-60/man/CS1422.htm#TopOfPage.

Conclusion

North Carolina law requires anyone who has cause to suspect that a child is abused or neglected to report the child's situation to the county department of social services. The law also requires reports about other children who need assistance or placement and children whose deaths may have been caused by maltreatment.

The protective services system, which includes mandated reporting, exists to carry out the state's policy of taking steps to ensure that every child has at least minimally adequate care. It is a safety net, designed to catch those children who have fallen—or are at risk of falling—below that minimal level. Obviously, people want more than that for their own and other children: protection from all kinds of harm; a level of care that is excellent, not just minimal; and opportunities to grow and develop to their full potential. Other systems do aim higher—education, health care, mental health services, and a host of other preventive and voluntary services. How adequately we provide services in areas like education, health care, child care, housing, substance abuse, and job training affects how many children and families need this safety net.

The reporting law is not designed to identify all children who are victims of maltreatment. Its focus is primarily on the care children receive from their parents or from custodians, guardians, or others whose roles resemble those of parents. Our society tolerates uninvited government intervention into families' lives only when absolutely necessary. The definitions that give the reporting law real meaning define the scope of permissible intervention.

Some people consider that threshold and scope insufficient in light of the number of children who are harmed by abuse or neglect. To others, state intervention may seem excessive, especially when based on a report that turns out to be unfounded.

The child protection system involves a delicate balance of societal values. It does not, and cannot, protect every child from harm or from the deprivations of inadequate care. It cannot operate at all, though, with respect to abused, neglected, and dependent children who never come to the attention of those with the legal authority and professional skills to intervene on their behalf. Having cause to suspect child abuse, neglect, or dependency and failing to report it is to risk pulling the safety net out from under a child. It is also to violate a legal responsibility that the North Carolina General Assembly has placed on every individual and institution in the state.

Appendix A. Articles 1 and 3 of the North Carolina Juvenile Code

This Appendix includes Articles 1 and 3 of the North Carolina Juvenile Code, Chapter 7B of the North Carolina General Statutes. The entire Juvenile Code is available online at www.ncga.state.nc.us/gascripts/Statutes/StatutesTOC.pl?Chapter=0007B.

Chapter 7B.

Juvenile Code.

SUBCHAPTER I. ABUSE, NEGLECT, DEPENDENCY.

Article 1.
Purposes; Definitions.

§ 7B-100. Purpose.

This Subchapter shall be interpreted and construed so as to implement the following purposes and policies:

(1) To provide procedures for the hearing of juvenile cases that assure fairness and equity and that protect the constitutional rights of juveniles and parents;

(2) To develop a disposition in each juvenile case that reflects consideration of the facts, the needs and limitations of the juvenile, and the strengths and weaknesses of the family.

(3) To provide for services for the protection of juveniles by means that respect both the right to family autonomy and the juveniles' needs for safety, continuity, and permanence; and

(4) To provide standards for the removal, when necessary, of juveniles from their homes and for the return of juveniles to their homes consistent with preventing the unnecessary or inappropriate separation of juveniles from their parents.

(5) To provide standards, consistent with the Adoption and Safe Families Act of 1997, P.L. 105-89, for ensuring that the best interests of the juvenile are of paramount consideration by the court and that when it is not in the juvenile's best interest to be returned home, the juvenile will be placed in a safe, permanent home within a reasonable amount of time.

§ 7B-101. Definitions.

As used in this Subchapter, unless the context clearly requires otherwise, the following words have the listed meanings:

(1) Abused juveniles. – Any juvenile less than 18 years of age whose parent, guardian, custodian, or caretaker:

    a. Inflicts or allows to be inflicted upon the juvenile a serious physical injury by other than accidental means;

    b. Creates or allows to be created a substantial risk of serious physical injury to the juvenile by other than accidental means;

    c. Uses or allows to be used upon the juvenile cruel or grossly inappropriate procedures or cruel or grossly inappropriate devices to modify behavior;

    d. Commits, permits, or encourages the commission of a violation of the following laws by, with, or upon the juvenile: first-degree rape, as provided in G.S. 14-27.2; rape of a child by an adult offender, as provided in G.S. 14-27.2A; second degree rape as provided in G.S. 14-27.3; first-degree sexual offense, as provided in G.S. 14-27.4; sexual offense with a child by an adult offender, as provided in G.S. 14-27.4A; second degree sexual offense, as provided in G.S. 14-27.5; sexual act by a custodian, as provided in G.S. 14-27.7; unlawful sale, surrender, or purchase of a minor, as provided in G.S. 14-43.14; crime against nature, as provided in G.S. 14-177; incest, as provided in G.S. 14-178; preparation of obscene photographs, slides, or motion pictures of the juvenile, as provided in G.S. 14-190.5; employing or permitting the juvenile to assist in a violation of the obscenity laws as provided in G.S. 14-190.6; dissemination of obscene material to the juvenile as provided in G.S. 14-190.7 and G.S. 14-190.8; displaying or disseminating material harmful to the juvenile as provided in G.S. 14-190.14 and G.S. 14-190.15; first and second degree sexual exploitation of the juvenile as provided in G.S. 14-190.16 and G.S. 14-190.17; promoting the prostitution of the juvenile as provided in G.S. 14-205.3(b); and taking indecent liberties with the juvenile, as provided in G.S. 14-202.1;

e. Creates or allows to be created serious emotional damage to the juvenile; serious emotional damage is evidenced by a juvenile's severe anxiety, depression, withdrawal, or aggressive behavior toward himself or others;

f. Encourages, directs, or approves of delinquent acts involving moral turpitude committed by the juvenile; or

g. Commits or allows to be committed an offense under G.S. 14-43.11 (human trafficking), G.S. 14-43.12 (involuntary servitude), or G.S. 14-43.13 (sexual servitude) against the child.

(2) Aggravated circumstances. – Any circumstance attending to the commission of an act of abuse or neglect which increases its enormity or adds to its injurious consequences, including, but not limited to, abandonment, torture, chronic abuse, or sexual abuse.

(3) Caretaker. – Any person other than a parent, guardian, or custodian who has responsibility for the health and welfare of a juvenile in a residential setting. A person responsible for a juvenile's health and welfare means a stepparent, foster parent, an adult member of the juvenile's household, an adult relative entrusted with the juvenile's care, any person such as a house parent or cottage parent who has primary responsibility for supervising a juvenile's health and welfare in a residential child care facility or residential educational facility, or any employee or volunteer of a division, institution, or school operated by the Department of Health and Human Services. "Caretaker" also means any person who has the responsibility for the care of a juvenile in a child care facility as defined in Article 7 of Chapter 110 of the General Statutes and includes any person who has the approval of the care provider to assume responsibility for the juveniles under the care of the care provider. Nothing in this subdivision shall be construed to impose a legal duty of support under Chapter 50 or Chapter 110 of the General Statutes. The duty imposed upon a caretaker as defined in this subdivision shall be for the purpose of this Subchapter only.

(4) Clerk. – Any clerk of superior court, acting clerk, or assistant or deputy clerk.

(5) Repealed by 2013-129, s. 1, effective October 1, 2013.

(6) Court. – The district court division of the General Court of Justice.

(7) Court of competent jurisdiction. – A court having the power and authority of law to act at the time of acting over the subject matter of the cause.

(7a) Criminal history. – A local, State, or federal criminal history of conviction or pending indictment of a crime, whether a misdemeanor or a felony, involving violence against a person.

(8) Custodian. – The person or agency that has been awarded legal custody of a juvenile by a court.

(9) Dependent juvenile. – A juvenile in need of assistance or placement because (i) the juvenile has no parent, guardian, or custodian responsible for the juvenile's care or supervision or (ii) the juvenile's parent, guardian, or custodian is unable to provide for the juvenile's care or supervision and lacks an appropriate alternative child care arrangement.

(10) Director. – The director of the county department of social services in the county in which the juvenile resides or is found, or the director's representative as authorized in G.S. 108A-14.

(11) District. – Any district court district as established by G.S. 7A-133.

(11a) Family assessment response. – A response to selected reports of child neglect and dependency as determined by the Director using a family-centered approach that is protection and prevention oriented and that evaluates the strengths and needs of the juvenile's family, as well as the condition of the juvenile.

(11b) Investigative assessment response. – A response to reports of child abuse and selected reports of child neglect and dependency as determined by the Director using a formal information gathering process to determine whether a juvenile is abused, neglected, or dependent.

(12) Judge. – Any district court judge.

(13) Judicial district. – Any district court district as established by G.S. 7A-133.

(14) Juvenile. – A person who has not reached the person's eighteenth birthday and is not married, emancipated, or a member of the Armed Forces of the United States.

(15) Neglected juvenile. – A juvenile who does not receive proper care, supervision, or discipline from the juvenile's parent, guardian, custodian, or caretaker; or who has been abandoned; or who is not provided necessary medical care; or who is not provided necessary remedial care; or who lives in an environment injurious to the juvenile's welfare; or who has been placed for care or adoption in violation of law. In determining whether a juvenile is a neglected juvenile, it is relevant whether that juvenile lives in a home where another juvenile has died as a result of suspected abuse or neglect or lives in a home where another juvenile has been subjected to abuse or neglect by an adult who regularly lives in the home.

(16) Petitioner. – The individual who initiates court action, whether by the filing of a petition or of a motion for review alleging the matter for adjudication.

(17) Prosecutor. – The district attorney or assistant district attorney assigned by the district attorney to juvenile proceedings.

(18) Reasonable efforts. – The diligent use of preventive or reunification services by a department of social services when a juvenile's remaining at home or returning home is consistent with achieving a safe, permanent home for the juvenile within a reasonable period of time. If a court of competent jurisdiction determines that the juvenile is not to be returned home, then reasonable efforts means the diligent and timely use of permanency planning services by a department of social services to develop and implement a permanent plan for the juvenile.

(18a) Responsible individual. – A parent, guardian, custodian, or caretaker who abuses or seriously neglects a juvenile.

(18b) Return home or reunification. – Placement of the juvenile in the home of either parent or placement of the juvenile in the home of a guardian or custodian from whose home the child was removed by court order.

(19) Safe home. – A home in which the juvenile is not at substantial risk of physical or emotional abuse or neglect.

(19a) Serious neglect. – Conduct, behavior, or inaction of the juvenile's parent, guardian, custodian, or caretaker that evidences a disregard of consequences of such magnitude that the conduct, behavior, or inaction constitutes an unequivocal danger to the juvenile's health, welfare, or safety, but does not constitute abuse.

(20) Repealed by 2013-129, s. 1, effective October 1, 2013.

(21) Substantial evidence. – Relevant evidence a reasonable mind would accept as adequate to support a conclusion.

(22) Working day. – Any day other than a Saturday, Sunday, or a legal holiday when the courthouse is closed for transactions.

The singular includes the plural, the masculine singular includes the feminine singular and masculine and feminine plural unless otherwise specified.

Article 3.
Screening of Abuse and Neglect Complaints.

§ 7B-300. Protective services.

The director of the department of social services in each county of the State shall establish protective services for juveniles alleged to be abused, neglected, or dependent.

Protective services shall include the screening of reports, the performance of an assessment using either a family assessment response or an investigative assessment response, casework, or other counseling services to parents, guardians, or other caretakers as provided by the director to help the parents, guardians, or other caretakers and the court to prevent abuse or neglect, to improve the quality of child care, to be more adequate parents, guardians, or caretakers, and to preserve and stabilize family life.

The provisions of this Article shall also apply to child care facilities as defined in G.S. 110-86.

§ 7B-301. Duty to report abuse, neglect, dependency, or death due to maltreatment.

(a) Any person or institution who has cause to suspect that any juvenile is abused, neglected, or dependent, as defined by G.S. 7B-101, or has died as the result of maltreatment, shall report the case of that juvenile to the director of the department of social services in the county where the juvenile resides or is found. The report may be made orally, by telephone, or in writing. The report shall include information as is known to the person making it including the name and address of the juvenile; the name and address of the juvenile's parent, guardian, or caretaker; the age of the juvenile; the names and ages of other juveniles in the home; the present whereabouts of the juvenile if not at the home address; the nature and extent of any injury or condition resulting from abuse, neglect, or dependency; and any other information which the person making the report believes might be helpful in establishing the need for protective services or court intervention. If the report is made orally or by telephone, the person making the report shall give the person's name, address, and telephone number. Refusal of the person making the report to give a name shall not preclude the department's assessment of the alleged abuse, neglect, dependency, or death as a result of maltreatment.

Upon receipt of any report of sexual abuse of the juvenile in a child care facility, the director shall notify the State Bureau of Investigation within 24 hours or on the next workday. If sexual abuse in a child care facility is not alleged in the initial report, but during the course of the assessment there is reason to suspect that sexual abuse has occurred, the director shall immediately notify the State Bureau of Investigation. Upon notification that sexual abuse may have occurred in a child care facility, the State Bureau of Investigation may form a task force to investigate the report.

(b) Any person or institution who knowingly or wantonly fails to report the case of a juvenile as required by subsection (a) of this section, or who knowingly or wantonly prevents another person from making a report as required by subsection (a) of this section, is guilty of a Class 1 misdemeanor.

(c) A director of social services who receives a report of sexual abuse of a juvenile in a child care facility and who knowingly fails to notify the State Bureau of Investigation of the report pursuant to subsection (a) of this section is guilty of a Class 1 misdemeanor.

[*Note*: S.L. 2013-52, sec. 7, added subsections (b) and (c) effective December 1, 2013.]

§ 7B-302. Assessment by director; access to confidential information; notification of person making the report.

(a) When a report of abuse, neglect, or dependency is received, the director of the department of social services shall make a prompt and thorough assessment, using either a family assessment response or an investigative assessment response, in order to ascertain the facts of the case, the extent of the abuse or neglect, and the risk of harm to the juvenile, in order to determine whether protective services should be provided or the complaint filed as a petition. When the report alleges abuse, the director shall immediately, but no later than 24 hours after receipt of the report, initiate the assessment. When the report alleges neglect or dependency, the director shall initiate the assessment within 72 hours following receipt of the report. When the report alleges abandonment, the director shall immediately initiate an assessment, take appropriate steps to assume temporary custody of the juvenile, and take appropriate steps to secure an order for nonsecure custody of the juvenile. The assessment and evaluation shall include a visit to the place where the juvenile resides, except when the report alleges abuse or neglect in a child care facility as defined in Article 7 of Chapter 110 of the General Statutes. When a report alleges abuse or neglect in a child care facility as defined in Article 7 of Chapter 110 of the General Statutes, a visit to the place where the juvenile resides is not required. When the report alleges abandonment, the assessment shall include a request from the director to law enforcement officials to investigate through the North Carolina Center for Missing Persons and other national and State resources whether the juvenile is a missing child.

(a1) All information received by the department of social services, including the identity of the reporter, shall be held in strictest confidence by the department, except under the following circumstances:

(1)   The department shall disclose confidential information to any federal, State, or local government entity or its agent in order to protect a juvenile from abuse or neglect. Any confidential information disclosed to any federal, State, or local government entity or its agent under this subsection shall remain confidential with the other government entity or its agent and shall only be redisclosed for purposes directly connected with carrying out that entity's mandated responsibilities.

(1a)   The department shall disclose confidential information regarding the identity of the reporter to any federal, State, or local government entity or its agent with a court order. The department may only disclose confidential information regarding the identity of the reporter to a federal, State, or local government entity or its agent without a court order when the entity demonstrates a need for the reporter's name to carry out the entity's mandated responsibilities.

(2) The information may be examined upon request by the juvenile's guardian ad litem or the juvenile, including a juvenile who has reached age 18 or been emancipated.

(3) A district or superior court judge of this State presiding over a civil matter in which the department of social services is not a party may order the department to release confidential information, after providing the department with reasonable notice and an opportunity to be heard and then determining that the information is relevant and necessary to the trial of the matter before the court and unavailable from any other source. This subdivision shall not be construed to relieve any court of its duty to conduct hearings and make findings required under relevant federal law, before ordering the release of any private medical or mental health information or records related to substance abuse or HIV status or treatment. The department of social services may surrender the requested records to the court, for in camera review, if the surrender is necessary to make the required determinations.

(4) A district or superior court judge of this State presiding over a criminal or delinquency matter shall conduct an in camera review prior to releasing to the defendant or juvenile any confidential records maintained by the department of social services, except those records the defendant or juvenile is entitled to pursuant to subdivision (2) of this subsection.

(5) The department may disclose confidential information to a parent, guardian, custodian, or caretaker in accordance with G.S. 7B-700 of this Subchapter.

(a2) If the director, at any time after receiving a report that a juvenile may be abused, neglected, or dependent, determines that the juvenile's legal residence is in another county, the director shall promptly notify the director in the county of the juvenile's residence, and the two directors shall coordinate efforts to ensure that appropriate actions are taken.

(b) When a report of a juvenile's death as a result of suspected maltreatment or a report of suspected abuse, neglect, or dependency of a juvenile in a noninstitutional setting is received, the director of the department of social services shall immediately ascertain if other juveniles live in the home, and, if so, initiate an assessment in order to determine whether they require protective services or whether immediate removal of the juveniles from the home is necessary for their protection. When a report of a juvenile's death as a result of maltreatment or a report of suspected abuse, neglect, or dependency of a juvenile in an institutional setting such as a residential child care facility or residential educational facility is received, the director of the department of social services shall immediately ascertain if other juveniles remain in the facility subject to the alleged perpetrator's care or supervision, and, if so, assess the circumstances of those juveniles in order to determine whether they require protective services or whether immediate removal of those juveniles from the facility is necessary for their protection.

(c) If the assessment indicates that abuse, neglect, or dependency has occurred, the director shall decide whether immediate removal of the juvenile or any other juveniles in the home is necessary for their protection. If immediate removal does not seem necessary, the director shall immediately provide or arrange for protective services. If the parent, guardian, custodian, or caretaker refuses to accept the protective services provided or arranged by the director, the director shall sign a petition seeking to invoke the jurisdiction of the court for the protection of the juvenile or juveniles.

(d) If immediate removal seems necessary for the protection of the juvenile or other juveniles in the home, the director shall sign a petition that alleges the applicable facts to invoke the jurisdiction of the court. Where the assessment shows that it is warranted, a protective services worker may assume temporary custody of the juvenile for the juvenile's protection pursuant to Article 5 of this Chapter.

(d1) Whenever a juvenile is removed from the home of a parent, guardian, custodian, stepparent, or adult relative entrusted with the juvenile's care due to physical abuse, the director shall conduct a thorough review of the background of the alleged abuser or abusers. This review shall include a criminal history check and a review of any available mental health records. If the review reveals that the alleged abuser or abusers have a history of violent behavior against people, the director shall petition the court to order the alleged abuser or abusers to submit to a complete mental health evaluation by a licensed psychologist or psychiatrist.

(e) In performing any duties related to the assessment of the report or the provision or arrangement for protective services, the director may consult with any public or private agencies or individuals, including the available State or local law enforcement officers who shall assist in the assessment and evaluation of the seriousness of any report of abuse, neglect, or dependency when requested by the director. The director or the director's representative may make a written demand for any information or reports, whether or not confidential, that may in the director's opinion be relevant to the assessment or provision of protective services. Upon the director's or the director's representative's request and unless protected by the attorney-client privilege, any public or private agency or individual shall provide access to and copies of this confidential information and these records to the extent permitted by federal law and regulations. If a custodian of criminal investigative information or records believes that release of the information will jeopardize the right of the State to prosecute a defendant or the right of a defendant to receive a fair trial or will undermine an ongoing or future investigation, it may seek an order from a court of competent jurisdiction to prevent disclosure of the information. In such an action, the custodian of the records shall have the burden of showing by a preponderance of the evidence that disclosure of the information in question will jeopardize the right of the State to prosecute a defendant or the right of a defendant to receive a fair trial or will undermine an ongoing or future investigation. Actions brought pursuant to this paragraph shall be set down for immediate hearing, and subsequent proceedings in the actions shall be accorded priority by the trial and appellate courts.

(f) Within five working days after receipt of the report of abuse, neglect, or dependency, the director shall give written notice to the person making the report, unless requested by that person not to give notice, as to whether the report was accepted for assessment and whether the report was referred to the appropriate State or local law enforcement agency.

(g) Within five working days after completion of the protective services assessment, the director shall give subsequent written notice to the person making the report, unless requested by that person not to give notice, as to whether there is a finding of abuse, neglect, or dependency, whether the county department of social services is taking action to protect the juvenile, and what action it is taking, including whether or not a petition was filed. The person making the report shall be informed of procedures necessary to request a review by the prosecutor of the director's decision not to file a petition. A request for review by the prosecutor shall be made within five working days of receipt of the second notification. The second notification shall include notice that, if the person making the report is not satisfied with the director's decision, the person may request review of the decision by the prosecutor within five working days of receipt. The person making the report may waive the person's right to this notification, and no notification is required if the person making the report does not identify himself to the director.

(h) The director or the director's representative may not enter a private residence for assessment purposes without at least one of the following:

(1) The reasonable belief that a juvenile is in imminent danger of death or serious physical injury.

(2) The permission of the parent or person responsible for the juvenile's care.

(3) The accompaniment of a law enforcement officer who has legal authority to enter the residence.

(4) An order from a court of competent jurisdiction.

§ 7B-303. Interference with assessment.

(a) If any person obstructs or interferes with an assessment required by G.S. 7B-302, the director may file a petition naming that person as respondent and requesting an order directing the respondent to cease the obstruction or interference. The petition shall contain the name and date of birth and address of the juvenile who is the subject of the assessment; shall include a concise statement of the basis for initiating the assessment, shall specifically describe the conduct alleged to constitute obstruction of or interference with the assessment; and shall be verified.

(b) For purposes of this section, obstruction of or interference with an assessment means refusing to disclose the whereabouts of the juvenile, refusing to allow the director to have personal access to the juvenile, refusing to allow the director to observe or interview the juvenile in private, refusing to allow the director access to confidential information and records upon request pursuant to G.S. 7B-302, refusing to allow the director to arrange for an evaluation of the juvenile by a physician or other expert, or other conduct that makes it impossible for the director to carry out the duty to assess the juvenile's condition.

(c) Upon filing of the petition, the court shall schedule a hearing to be held not less than five days after service of the petition and summons on the respondent. Service of the petition and summons and notice of hearing shall be made as provided by the Rules of Civil Procedure on the respondent; the juvenile's parent, guardian, custodian, or caretaker; and any other person determined by the court to be a necessary party. If at the hearing on the petition the court finds by clear, cogent, and convincing evidence that the respondent, without lawful excuse, has obstructed or interfered with an assessment required by G.S. 7B-302, the court may order the respondent to cease such obstruction or interference. The burden of proof shall be on the petitioner.

(d) If the director has reason to believe that the juvenile is in need of immediate protection or assistance, the director shall so allege in the petition and may seek an ex parte order from the court. If the court, from the verified petition and any inquiry the court makes of the director, finds probable cause to believe both that the juvenile is at risk of immediate harm and that the respondent is obstructing or interfering with the director's ability to assess the juvenile's condition, the court may enter an ex parte order directing the respondent to cease the obstruction or interference. The order shall be limited to provisions necessary to enable the director to conduct an assessment sufficient to determine whether the juvenile is in need of immediate protection or assistance. Within 10 days after the entry of an ex parte order under this subsection, a hearing shall be held to determine whether there is good cause for the continuation of the order or the entry of a different order. An order entered under this subsection shall be served on the respondent along with a copy of the petition, summons, and notice of hearing.

(e) The director may be required at a hearing under this section to reveal the identity of any person who made a report of suspected abuse, neglect, or dependency as required by G.S. 7B-301.

(f) An order entered pursuant to this section is enforceable by civil or criminal contempt as provided in Chapter 5A of the General Statutes.

§ 7B-304: Repealed by Session Laws 2003, c. 140, s. 1, effective June 4, 2003.

§ 7B-305. Request for review by prosecutor.

The person making the report shall have five working days, from receipt of the decision of the director of the department of social services not to petition the court, to notify the prosecutor that the person is requesting a review. The prosecutor shall notify the person making the report and the director of the time and place for the review, and the director shall immediately transmit to the prosecutor a copy of a summary of the assessment.

§ 7B-306. Review by prosecutor.

The prosecutor shall review the director's determination that a petition should not be filed within 20 days after the person making the report is notified. The review shall include conferences with the person making the report, the protective services worker, the juvenile, if practicable, and other persons known to have pertinent information about the juvenile or the juvenile's family. At the conclusion of the conferences, the prosecutor may affirm the decision made by the director, may request the appropriate local law enforcement agency to investigate the allegations, or may direct the director to file a petition.

§ 7B-307. Duty of director to report evidence of abuse, neglect; investigation by local law enforcement; notification of Department of Health and Human Services and State Bureau of Investigation.

(a) If the director finds evidence that a juvenile may have been abused as defined by G.S. 7B-101, the director shall make an immediate oral and subsequent written report of the findings to the district attorney or the district attorney's designee and the appropriate local law enforcement agency within 48 hours after receipt of the report. The local law enforcement agency shall immediately, but no later than 48 hours after receipt of the information, initiate and coordinate a criminal investigation with the protective services assessment being conducted by the county department of social services. Upon completion of the investigation, the district attorney shall determine whether criminal prosecution is appropriate and may request the director or the director's designee to appear before a magistrate.

If the director receives information that a juvenile may have been physically harmed in violation of any criminal statute by any person other than the juvenile's parent, guardian, custodian, or caretaker, the director shall make an immediate oral and subsequent written report of that information to the district attorney or the district attorney's designee and to the appropriate local law enforcement agency within 48 hours after receipt of the information. The local law enforcement agency shall immediately, but no later than 48 hours after receipt of the information, initiate a criminal investigation. Upon completion of the investigation, the district attorney shall determine whether criminal prosecution is appropriate.

If the report received pursuant to G.S. 7B-301 involves abuse or neglect of a juvenile in child care, the director shall notify the Department of Health and Human Services within 24 hours or on the next working day of receipt of the report.

(b) If the director finds evidence that a juvenile has been abused or neglected as defined by G.S. 7B-101 in a child care facility, the director shall immediately so notify the Department of Health and Human Services and, in the case of sexual abuse, the State Bureau of Investigation, in such a way as does not violate the law guaranteeing the confidentiality of the records of the department of social services.

(c) Upon completion of the assessment, the director shall give the Department written notification of the results of the assessment required by G.S. 7B-302. Upon completion of an assessment of sexual abuse in a child care facility, the director shall also make written notification of the results of the assessment to the State Bureau of Investigation.

The director of the department of social services shall submit a report of alleged abuse, neglect, or dependency cases or child fatalities that are the result of alleged maltreatment to the central registry under the policies adopted by the Social Services Commission.

§ 7B-308. Authority of medical professionals in abuse cases.

(a) Any physician or administrator of a hospital, clinic, or other medical facility to which a suspected abused juvenile is brought for medical diagnosis or treatment shall have the right, when authorized by the chief district court judge of the district or the judge's designee, to retain physical custody of the juvenile in the facility when the physician who examines the juvenile certifies in writing that the juvenile who is suspected of being abused should remain for medical treatment or that, according to the juvenile's medical evaluation, it is unsafe for the juvenile to return to the juvenile's parent, guardian, custodian, or caretaker. This written certification must be signed by the certifying physician and must include the time and date that the judicial authority to retain custody is given. Copies of the written certification must be appended to the juvenile's medical and judicial records and another copy must be given to the juvenile's parent, guardian, custodian, or caretaker. The right to retain custody in the facility shall exist for up to 12 hours from the time and date contained in the written certification.

(b) Immediately upon receipt of judicial authority to retain custody, the physician, the administrator, or that person's designee shall so notify the director of social services for the county in which the facility is located. The director shall treat this notification as a report of suspected abuse and shall immediately begin an assessment of the case.

(1) If the assessment reveals (i) that it is the opinion of the certifying physician that the juvenile is in need of medical treatment to cure or alleviate physical distress or to prevent the juvenile from suffering serious physical injury, and (ii) that it is the opinion of the physician that the juvenile should for these reasons remain in the custody of the facility for 12 hours, but (iii) that the juvenile's parent, guardian, custodian, or caretaker cannot be reached or, upon request, will not consent to the treatment within the facility, the director shall within the initial 12-hour period file a juvenile petition alleging abuse and setting forth supporting allegations and shall seek a nonsecure custody order. A petition filed and a nonsecure custody order obtained in accordance with this subdivision shall come on for hearing under the regular provisions of this Subchapter unless the director and the certifying physician together voluntarily dismiss the petition.

(2) In all cases except those described in subdivision (1) above, the director shall conduct the assessment and may initiate juvenile proceedings and take all other steps authorized by the regular provisions of this Subchapter. If the director decides not to file a petition, the physician, the administrator, or that person's designee may ask the prosecutor to review this decision according to the provisions of G.S. 7B-305 and G.S. 7B-306.

(c) If, upon hearing, the court determines that the juvenile is found in a county other than the county of legal residence, in accord with G.S. 153A-257, the juvenile may be transferred, in accord with G.S. 7B-903(2), to the custody of the department of social services in the county of residence.

(d) If the court, upon inquiry, determines that the medical treatment rendered was necessary and appropriate, the cost of that treatment may be charged to the parents, guardian, custodian, or caretaker, or, if the parents are unable to pay, to the county of residence in accordance with G.S. 7B-903 and G.S. 7B-904.

(e) Except as otherwise provided, a petition begun under this section shall proceed in like manner with petitions begun under G.S. 7B-302.

(f) The procedures in this section are in addition to, and not in derogation of, the abuse and neglect reporting provisions of G.S. 7B-301 and the temporary custody provisions of G.S. 7B-500. Nothing in this section shall preclude a physician or administrator and a director of social services from following the procedures of G.S. 7B-301 and G.S. 7B-500 whenever these procedures are more appropriate to the juvenile's circumstances.

§ 7B-309. Immunity of persons reporting and cooperating in an assessment.

Anyone who makes a report pursuant to this Article, cooperates with the county department of social services in a protective services assessment, testifies in any judicial proceeding resulting from a protective services report or assessment, or otherwise participates in the program authorized by this Article, is immune from any civil or criminal liability that might otherwise be incurred or imposed for that action provided that the person was acting in good faith. In any proceeding involving liability, good faith is presumed.

§ 7B-310. Privileges not grounds for failing to report or for excluding evidence.

No privilege shall be grounds for any person or institution failing to report that a juvenile may have been abused, neglected, or dependent, even if the knowledge or suspicion is acquired in an official professional capacity, except when the knowledge or suspicion is gained by an attorney from that attorney's client during representation only in the abuse, neglect, or dependency case. No privilege, except the attorney-client privilege, shall be grounds for excluding evidence of abuse, neglect, or dependency in any judicial proceeding (civil, criminal, or juvenile) in which a juvenile's abuse, neglect, or dependency is in issue nor in any judicial proceeding resulting from a report submitted under this Article, both as this privilege relates to the competency of the witness and to the exclusion of confidential communications.

§ 7B-311. Central registry; responsible individuals list.

(a) The Department of Health and Human Services shall maintain a central registry of abuse, neglect, and dependency cases and child fatalities that are the result of alleged maltreatment that are reported under this Article in order to compile data for appropriate study of the extent of abuse and neglect within the State and to identify repeated abuses of the same juvenile or of other juveniles in the same family. This data shall be furnished by county directors of social services to the Department of Health and Human Services and shall be confidential, subject to rules adopted by the Social Services Commission providing for its use for study and research and for other appropriate disclosure. Data shall not be used at any hearing or court proceeding unless based upon a final judgment of a court of law.

(b) The Department shall also maintain a list of responsible individuals. The Department may provide information from this list to child caring institutions, child placing agencies, group home facilities, and other providers of foster care, child care, or adoption services that need to determine the fitness of individuals to care for or adopt children. The name of an individual who has been identified as a responsible individual shall be placed on the responsible individuals list only after one of the following:

(1) The individual is properly notified pursuant to G.S. 7B-320 and fails to file a petition for judicial review in a timely manner.

(2) The court determines that the individual is a responsible individual as a result of a hearing on the individual's petition for judicial review.

(3) The individual is criminally convicted as a result of the same incident involved in an investigative assessment response.

(c) It is unlawful for any public official or public employee to knowingly and willfully release information from either the central registry or the responsible individuals list to a person who is not authorized to receive the information. It is unlawful for any person who is authorized to receive information from the central registry or the responsible individuals list to release that information to an unauthorized person. It is unlawful for any person who is not authorized to receive information from the central registry or the responsible individuals list to access or attempt to access that information. A person who commits an offense described in this subsection is guilty of a Class 3 misdemeanor.

(d) The Social Services Commission shall adopt rules regarding the operation of the central registry and responsible individuals list, including procedures for each of the following:

(1) Filing data.

(2) Notifying an individual that the individual has been determined by the director to be a responsible individual.

(3) Correcting and expunging information.

(4) Determining persons who are authorized to receive information from the responsible individuals list.

(5) Releasing information from the responsible individuals list to authorized requestors.

(6) Gathering statistical information.

(7) Keeping and maintaining information placed in the registry and on the responsible individuals list.

(8) Repealed by Session Laws 2010-90, s. 4, effective July 11, 2010.

§§ 7B-312 through 7B-319: Reserved for future codification purposes.

Appendix B. Selected Internet Sites

North Carolina—Governmental

County Departments of Social Services (contact information)
www.ncacdss.org/counties.html

N.C. Department of Health and Human Services
www.dhhs.state.nc.us

> State DHHS Manuals
> http://info.dhhs.state.nc.us/olm/manuals/default.aspx

N.C. Division of Social Services
www.dhhs.state.nc.us/dss

> About Child Abuse and Neglect
> www.ncdhhs.gov/dss/cps/about.htm

> All manuals issued by the State Division of Social Services
> http://info.dhhs.state.nc.us/olm/manuals/manuals.aspx?dc=dss

> Child Protective Services Manual
> http://info.dhhs.state.nc.us/olm/manuals/dss/csm-60/man

> Forms issued by the State Division of Social Services
> http://info.dhhs.state.nc.us/olm/forms/forms.aspx?dc=dss

Jordan Institute for Families, UNC School of Social Work
http://ssw.unc.edu/jordan

> Child Welfare Statistics
> Duncan, D.F., Kum, H.C., Flair, K.A., Stewart, C.J., Vaughn, J., Bauer, R.,
> and You, A. (2012). "Management Assistance for Child Welfare, Work
> First, and Food & Nutrition Services in North Carolina." UNC at Chapel
> Hill Jordan Institute for Families.
> http://ssw.unc.edu/ma

North Carolina General Assembly
www.ncleg.net

> North Carolina General Statutes
> www.ncleg.net/gascripts/Statutes/StatutesTOC.pl

> North Carolina Juvenile Code
> www.ncleg.net/gascripts/Statutes/StatutesTOC.pl?Chapter=0007B

North Carolina Administrative Code (N.C.A.C.)
http://ncrules.state.nc.us/ncadministrativ_/default.htm

> Health and Human Services – Children's Services [10A N.C.A.C. 70]
> http://ncrules.state.nc.us/ncac.asp?folderName=\Title 10A - Health and
> Human Services\Chapter 70 - Children's Services

North Carolina Court System
www.nccourts.org

> Guardian Ad Litem Program
> www.nccourts.org/Citizens/GAL/Default.asp

> Office of Parent Representation
> www.ncids.org/ParentRepresentation/index.html

> Court Improvement Program (CIP)
> www.nccourts.org/Citizens/CPrograms/Improvement/Default.asp

> Family Court
> www.nccourts.org/Citizens/CPrograms/Family/Default.asp

> N.C. Appellate Court Opinions
> www.aoc.state.nc.us/www/public/html/opinions.htm

North Carolina—Non-Governmental

Prevent Child Abuse North Carolina
www.preventchildabusenc.org/index.cfm?fuseaction=cms.home

> Web-based Training: Recognizing and Responding to Suspicions of
> Child Maltreatment
> www.preventchildabusenc.org/index.cfm?fuseaction=cms.page&id=1047

Action for Children North Carolina
www.ncchild.org

Child Advocacy Centers of North Carolina
www.cacnc.org/home

The Covenant with North Carolina's Children
www.nccovenant.org

Duke Center for Child and Family Policy
www.childandfamilypolicy.duke.edu

Federal and National

Federal Child Welfare and Reporting Laws

> Indian Child Protection and Family Violence Prevention Act,
> 25 U.S.C. Chapter 34 (§§ 3201–3211)
> www.law.cornell.edu/uscode/text/25/chapter-34

> Victims of Child Abuse, 42 U.S.C. Chapter 132 (§§ 13001–13055)
> www.law.cornell.edu/uscode/text/42/chapter-132

U.S. Department of Health and Human Services
www.hhs.gov

> DHHS Administration for Children and Families
> www.acf.hhs.gov/index.html

> Children's Bureau
> www.acf.hhs.gov/programs/cb

> Child Welfare Information Gateway
> www.childwelfare.gov

> National Child Welfare Resource Center on Legal and Judicial Issues
> www.abanet.org/abanet/child/home.cfm

ABA Center on Children and the Law
www.abanet.org/child/home2.html

> ABA Publication *Child Law Practice*
> www.abanet.org/child/clp

American Professional Society on the Abuse of Children
www.apsac.org

National Council of Juvenile and Family Court Judges
www.ncjfcj.org

American Academy of Pediatrics, Section on Child Abuse and Neglect
www2.aap.org/sections/childabuseneglect

American Humane Association
www.americanhumane.org/children

National Family Preservation Network
www.nfpn.org

Child Abuse Prevention Network
www.child-abuse.com

Children's Defense Fund
www.childrensdefense.org/index.htm

National Association of Counsel for Children
www.naccchildlaw.org

National CASA (Court Appointed Special Advocate)
http://nationalcasa.org

National Center for Youth Law
www.youthlaw.org

National Data Archive on Child Abuse and Neglect, Family Life Development Center, College of Human Ecology, Cornell University
www.ndacan.cornell.edu

Prevent Child Abuse America
www.preventchildabuse.org